# One Thing at a Time

*The Art of Presence in a World Out to Lunch*

Heather Ralston

Copyright © 2023 Heather Ralston

All rights reserved.

ISBN: 9798865850779

# DEDICATION

To those who make the hard choices: you are seen.
To those who have lost their support structures: you are loved.
To those who remain soft and kind: it matters.
To humanity: you possess within you all the love that beats all hearts, and the capacity to act as such.

# CONTENTS

Introduction — i

1 - Knowing Your Journey — 1

2 - Unlearning from Unteachers — 24

3 - The "Other" — 36

4 - Taking Responsibility — 49

5 - The Deep Dive into Love — 55

6 - Groundwork - Coming Clean — 66

7 - The Ultimate Surrender — 86

8 - Knowing and Doing What You Want — 114

9 - Exercises — 126

10 - One Thing at a Time — 145

# INTRODUCTION

Seventeen years ago, the most terrifying thing in life was the mind called "mine." After twenty years, this mind had stacked memory after memory to be recalled at will, dragging the body along for the ride. As a result, this physical body exhibited symptoms of what we call acid reflux, swollen ankles, spider veins, digestive issues, migraine and tension headaches, frequent illness, tightness in the chest, heart palpitations, and debilitating anxiety, not to mention various other transient symptoms. After a series of events I had deemed traumatic, it seemed one final straw had finally broken the camel's back - my mind raced from thought to thought, and any attempt to slow or cease the flow only caused it to rage more strongly out of control. Though I had never meditated and really had no interest in the activity, the suffering had grown so intense that I would do anything to be free of it. When I sat down to meditate, a sense of terror quickly overtook me - I could not stop my thoughts, this technique didn't seem like it was going to offer relief any time soon, and I began to wonder how much longer I could endure.

It was then that, for the first time in my life, I faced the demons that had accumulated through my mother's four marriages, around seventeen home relocations by the time I was eighteen, playing the part of an overachiever perfectionist, and generally being part of a contentious and highly suppressed family dynamic where real love was so often seemingly covered over by fear, all of this culminating with the death of my mother just after I left for college. In all this, I learned every way to survive yet not a single skill that could help me in managing stress, and suppressed emotions were reaching a boiling point with regularity. In order to get by, I learned just enough to stop the boiling. These small lessons were integrated into my personality by the part of me that loved to be distinguished from others - ego - telling myself that now I was "evolved," I had overcome a supposed anxiety disorder, calmed my acid reflux, regulated my bowels, the swelling in my ankles disappeared, and even those spider veins stopped their crawling. It seemed I had figured out the secret to life, and yet there was still plentiful suffering in my experience.

Ten years ago, as part of my ongoing efforts to release the past, I began writing the story of my life in the hope that seeing it from a new perspective would help me work through all that had happened. It seemed quite therapeutic, seeing myself in the third person and able to apply compassion that I wouldn't have given myself otherwise. I was also able to identify some self-imposed limitations and work through them. As I wrote my own story, I would often weep, recognizing areas where I had suppressed emotions and hidden memories from myself. Through this process and as life continued to unfold, I began to see that my story and insights might help others who had been through similar things or were struggling in a similar way. With that, I began to take the idea of publishing this writing seriously for the first time.

I have spent the past decade writing a story that has continually morphed into something new - just as I was wrapping up a draft, I would realize I had moved past the way of thinking that had informed it, and began re-writing. Each time, it seemed the story aspect took up less and less space, making way for the insights that continued to come and the ways in which they were brought on. As the ego began to recede into the background, only the parts of my story which were instructive interested me.

Recently, I realized what and who I really am after a seventeen year journey. This realization, spurred on from a desire to be free of suffering, ironically has nothing to do with the character Heather and her churnings - in fact, as we will discuss, the wording that is typically used to describe these experiences is insufficient in conveying the true meaning of this realization. Though not yet completely integrated and continually unfolding, this realization led to one final and decisive re-write. I have noticed that aspects of the story of Heather and of the past in general are no longer being held onto - they are being released from memory as I give less space to the past and future, and as these memories are deemed unhelpful. All along this journey, The Book has been my companion and guide.

When I read the words of Thich Nhat Han around fifteen years ago, took in his guidance to take one step at a time, one breath at a time, and to do the dishes with one's full attention, the mind took the advice to be overly simplistic and out of touch with the Western mind. How was I ever going to focus solely on dishes when I had a full-time job, went to school full-time, and was grappling with *real* trauma? How would I ever focus on one single breath without encroaching thoughts when I seemingly had no family support and lived in such a dangerous world? I didn't realize that not only were these thoughts entirely false, his words were incredibly profound, overlooked in their simplicity, and the complete heart of zen, yoga, nonduality, and of the effortless arising of the continuous present moment. I never would have guessed I would write a book centered around this. I never would have thought this could be the key to overcoming all suffering.

The goal of this work, such as it is, is to allow it to join the myriad voices of teachers before me - not because I have unearthed some new idea that has never been discovered before, but because as the mind evolves, so must the message and the teacher, so that at any time the answer to the question "how many more books on self-realization do we need" will be "at least one more, and also none." In a time when the sacred seems to be absent, actively suppressed, or weaponized and commercialized in general society, in a time when politics and other media seem to be driving us into further and further unconsciousness, we must recognize that the collective state of unconsciousness has brought humanity to this point and that for this practical problem, an updated "spiritual" solution is absolutely essential. Until such time as enough humans have become liberated from this state of suffering to liberate the collective, teams of teachers put forth new works written in new ways, relating timeless messages to newer and newer happenings and matching the sentiment of the mind, all from the effortless place of knowing that all has been and always will be well. This strange paradox and others I hope to shed light on in this contribution to and from the world's library of wisdom, filtered through and for the dense Western mind. I am delighted to take this journey with you.

# CHAPTER ONE

## KNOWING YOUR JOURNEY

Ah, humanity... the marvels we've accomplished. We've got pyramids, alloyed metal, our pets are microchipped... there's nothing we can't achieve! And yet, somehow, we've all but submitted to the consensus that we are less happy than we've ever been. Somehow, the minds that have conjured these advancements also seem to be maladapted to the kind of society that has prioritized and facilitated the growth of the mind through these pursuits. We can't sleep, can't process what we eat, don't want to be around other minds or let them near ours, and many of us simply can't stand the mind we have. What could we possibly be doing that is so fundamentally wrong? Potential answers abound.

"The Bhagavad Gita," written between 200 BCE and 200 CE, describes the process of coming to know the true nature of reality as "the journey of the self, through the self, to the self." The author was referring to the yogic path - however, awakened humans the world over have come to see that the methods one employs on their journey all fit this description. It may seem rather cryptic, like so many things within the realm of what we've called "spirituality" - but it's pretty straightforward. When one realizes that they no longer wish to experience suffering as they have, they begin to look more closely at the contents of the self they've constructed - the beliefs, values, opinions, and thoughts they seem to hold dear. When they take a good look at these things, asking what is real and what is subjective, open to interpretation, unverifiable, or outright false, the content of the mind, the stuff we call "me," starts falling away, leaving only what is absolutely true - the understanding of one's true nature. But is this really all there is to a journey so important, a process we have decided must be complicated, arduous, and lifelong?

On this journey to the true self, we are not talking about this small constructed self, the glorified filing cabinet full of your teachers' voices, your favorite band based on your ever-evolving idea of where you fall within a societal hierarchy, and those things the neighbor kids told you that your five-year-old self believed which somehow stuck around in the subconscious, controlling your actions and reactions to this day. We are talking about the true Self - what is left when the thoughts, feelings, and sensations fall away.

The Great Questions have persisted throughout our time on this earth for good reason. The answer to these questions (yes, there is one answer to all the questions), though laughably simple when we get it, is not going to seem simple at first. It cannot be understood by the human mind, and that's about all you've used to get around so far. The mind, ironically and poetically akin to a computer working with ones and zeros, isn't going to understand the Infinite, for which there are no concepts. If you've experienced contemplating deep space or the amount of money making up the national debt, you know that the machine you're experiencing has some very real limitations.

This is because, by nature, the very mind that may be pointlessly reading this text out loud to itself is also quite finite, subject to imperfection, and currently being asked to do work it wasn't designed for. It's like asking a computer to explain love, or expecting a robot to function outside of its programming - it can only recite facts and stick to rules.

If that isn't enough, the mind was designed not to understand the Infinite *on purpose*. As you will come to see, the game of life has been designed this way with one goal in mind, and in order to reach that goal, we are playing the game of working with exactly the bodies and minds we have access to.

Because the attempts to understand something a mind simply cannot understand are endlessly futile, this leaves but one option: we must go beyond the mind. Go ahead and try, I'll wait. Out of habit, the attempt to understand this will begin with a mind searching for what it cannot know, still filtering all information through itself, using it to build itself up even further by telling itself things like, "look how smart I am for remembering and even regurgitating this complex idea, I can't wait for my enemies to find out how witty and wise I'm becoming." Eventually, when through some series of events or other there is the capacity to see a deeper resonance from a place beyond the mind for the first time, this is when our journey really gets its wings. When the mind is sufficiently checked just enough to recede into the background of experience, when the voice in the head is silent for just a moment or when attention can be diverted from that to what is really unfolding, the true Self shows itself. Only then will you realize why words never worked, concepts made things muddy, and your mind played dodgeball night and day, especially when you were on the brink of a breakthrough. If, like this character called Heather (and also "me"), you find yourself overcome with suffering and prepared to do almost anything to make this journey short and sweet, it is important to know this and all the other things you're up against.

### What is Spiritual?

It will help a great deal if you are able to see this as something beyond a spiritual experience - in fact, not to place that label on this experience at all. It is simply the quest to understand the true nature of things through direct experience. If the true nature of things ends up fitting the definition of the human-made concept called "spiritual," then so be it - but placing such a label tends to give the mind leave to box in our experience - it must seemingly be filled with incense, patchouli, flowing skirts, linen pants, soft smiles, and gurus if it is to be authentic. In fact, labeling as such could add years of detours in the form of building up experiences in the mind - "when I become enlightened I will see colors with my eyes closed, experience 'god,' be infallible, never experience pain again" - all of these are going to delay understanding. Expecting the journey to be "good vibes only" means you will be avoiding your own darkness and in fear of others' struggles, and our goal here is to avoid nothing - to look honestly at life. I have often encountered individuals calling themselves "spiritual" who are not embarking upon any deeper journey but rather have decided to study crystals, astrology, and aromatherapy - all quite interesting, but all pertaining to the physical aspect of our experience. In reality, what we are doing on this journey is learning what we already are without all of that, and that doesn't require any special practices or big changes. The mind's fear is often that we will lose some aspect of ourselves, be less fun, or unbox some mystery we would rather not know, but this is based on a false belief that the mysterious is dangerous and an attachment to whatever we've already decided about the world. If that wasn't enough, it seems we must also dive into the mysteries of existence without upsetting the apple cart of society. If we want to go beyond all that human beings have established on this earth, certainly a journey which fits into societal expectations is going to be limited - and in its limitation, there will be much less opportunity to gain the insight that only arises when you are willing to be completely honest. In other words - you're going to have to let go of hogwash if you hope to go beyond the mind, and there's quite a lot of it. In the end, realization of the true self, and learning to access the peace that comes with that, is very simple. Just a slight recalibration in view will do it, like going from wearing bifocals to contacts or removing a self-imposed gloom filter from your life's camera lens. I say this, and yet your mind may endlessly attempt to throw up obstacles, saying "this can't possibly be easy or everyone would know," "this thing you just said is too simple to contain the very Truth of existence," and so on. As you will come to see, there is a reason for thinking this way, and it's okay. It's also time to be done with it. You could spend years in this thought loop before an insight dawns on you if you are not willing to question every single thought you notice.

At times in this work, reference will be made to different traditions as having grasped or referred to this in one way or another. Similarly "spiritual" words and concepts may be used to convey a point. The words and concepts may be borrowed from religions and traditions, simply because they have been found to be effective pointers or their equivalent does not exist in another language. It is incredibly powerful to realize that what we call self-realization shares outcomes with the Buddhist concept of becoming nobody or the Christian ideas of dying to the self or being born again.

First, it is important to note that we are not merely combining genres to create some kind of new spin on spirituality. All traditions were borne of the exact same urge within humans to reach for the Infinite, to patch up a seemingly broken existence, and the only thing separating those traditions is interpretation and perception. Every single human, in their vain efforts to be happy, is cooperating in the process of mass seeking to bridge the gap between the form and the formless, whether this is known or not. As the late teacher Ram Dass said, *we are all walking each other home*. It is only the sense that these things are fundamentally different that allows any concept of conflict ever to arise - the coming pages will illustrate this in detail. Together, we are going to become okay with the questioning of all that the mind holds most dear - to release that which is not verifiably, universally true, and yet has simultaneously comforted and tortured the mind for a significant portion of your time experiencing this body. Today, we are ready to go beyond the illusory divides, to let go of "should," "good," "bad," obligatory morality, clinging to pleasure, and aversion to life unfolding as it is currently. For most of human history, a quest of this kind has entailed going out into the world seeking truth, only to realize that universal truth is a pinch of this, a pinch of that, and ultimately throwing it all off a cliff, leaving a cleansed, all-knowing, and blissful stillness. Now, we have the ability to go straight to the source of that Knowing without all the detours. This journey is not for special people - it is not for "spiritual" people, or for "joiners." These labels don't point to real things, but to present perceptions of oneself and others. The journey to a deeper understanding of life may seem spiritual for a time because that is the way the mind is accustomed to thinking about it, and the human apparatus is fully capable of seeing life through a filter which only allows in what confirms belief and comfort. Suddenly, the whole point of all this will reveal itself as the most obvious of things, something that has been right in front of us every moment. Our ability to remain agile, not to reduce this journey to mere human constructs and not to be hung up on anything which defies our present understanding, determines the ease with which we will come to remember ultimate and effortless peace - in fact, to realize that it was never forgotten.

    I realize now that my own Christian experience in early life led me to a faith which allowed the mind to recede in this effortless way. I had genuine "holy moments" both at church and alone, when staring at trees and observing the intelligence in their design, when hearing the sound of many voices singing in harmony in my high school choir or on Sunday mornings. In these moments, all was well, all was one, fear disappeared, and everything made sense. I did not need to be told that all was one - I knew it beyond even the cells of the body. At that time, these experiences were twisted up in a concept of god, of something outside of me I was told was male and vengeful, and they had not yet been tested by the more intense tragedies of the human experience - but the mechanism of dropping the mind in an act of faith was genuine. Because of these blissful moments, I believed my understanding at that time to be "it." For the Christian who has a genuine relationship with their higher power, that is the feeling that keeps one going on their journey. There is one major way I will introduce within this book in which Universal truth semantically differs from the popular interpretation of Christianity: that god who created the world, whose presence brings rise to the well-known peace which passes all understanding and which is knowingly experienced at certain moments in life, is not male, does not resemble a human, is not vengeful, does not judge, and does not conform to most of the ideas we have attached to the word and concept "god." That so-called deity is our true identity, and the true identity and source of all living things.

**You VS. Conditioning**

Everything you have just read may fly in the face of all you have ever been told. If so, you may still be in for quite a ride. That is because you have experienced a completely unformed mind absorbing concepts and conditioning ever since it assigned "ba-ba" to "bottle." You have witnessed the mind as a dry sponge surrounded by people dropping survival-flavored water all over it. As the mind grows in content and intensity and the sense of the way things are solidifies, there is less and less room for more water in that sponge. By the time you experience adulthood, that mind may have very little interest in taking in any new or differing information, especially if that conditioning brought with it experiences that have led to lack of trust, or there is enough comfort and complacency to make veering off the path not yet worth it. You might notice resentment toward those who taught you, a resistance to being manipulated for societal ends "yet again," or a fear of losing what you've supposedly managed to secure.

Rest assured, the work you are undertaking is the furthest thing from that - indeed, in the end it isn't even work. However, it will require a heroic level of openness, accountability, and courage in the short-term. Even when we rest on a foundation made completely of sand, we are generally blindsided when it is pulled out from under us - the mind is quite capable of creating all sorts of mental scenarios to scare itself back into old beliefs as though our very life depends upon it. My own experience in this area was quite terrifying at the time, though I know now that I was never in any danger. The mind, completely intertwined with the body, creates sensations in the body which mimic ill health or impending death in order to scare itself away from precisely the thing required to move beyond suffering. It's a tricky thing, nigh impossible (and yet, in the end, entirely effortless and simple), and this means you will also need a great deal of compassion.

**Cease to Cherish Opinions**

As you will learn on this journey, and as a formative role model from my childhood loves to plagiarize from Salt N Pepa, "opinions are like assholes; everybody's got one." When I think about the power of opinion, I love to think of a close childhood companion, just beginning to grapple with logic and learning to use it to her benefit. When her mother said her makeup was "too adult" and she couldn't continue to wear it that way, she replied, "well, that's your opinion." She would also play this the opposite way - when told she was wrong, she would attempt to cover herself by proclaiming, "well, it's my opinion." The simple manipulation such a young mind was already capable of, at different times either inflating or deflating the importance to suit her needs, has always made me laugh inwardly whenever I think of it. However, this is an excellent example of the state of the world, especially as these minds begin to grasp more and more subtle forms of this way of manipulating and fooling themselves.

In reality, opinions get us nowhere - they are completely pointless figments of the mind which it stands on when taking issue with basically everything. If it simply abstained from this, what do you think would remain? How do you feel when you consider what life would be like if the mind were silent?

The fact that human beings even form opinions is a side effect of social conditioning - for thousands of years, humans have been developing more and more complicated ideas about what is good and bad in the world, with "bad" as applied to a human sometimes encountering harsh critique and even the removal of one's bodily autonomy through medication or imprisonment for the supposed safety of the collective. We know in retrospect just how wrong public opinion proved to be in many of those situations, and we can see this as a tribal remnant filled with superstition - "these left handed people/ this type of berry/ these anarchists not contributing as much to the GDP are going to get us all killed out here!" Meanwhile, the non-human members of the animal kingdom are out there with no sense of morality and no fear or shame, except our anxious domesticated friends, about as mal-adapted to sedentary and indoor lives as humans are. In other words, all aspects of morality originated in the human mind, and it's the only species subject to following the ideas of "good" and "evil" - perhaps this rings a biblical bell in our memories, and perhaps our understanding of "the knowledge of good and evil" will strike a different chord as we read on.

Humanity is also the only species to have invented the concept of the "problem," and the only ones who truly suffer. To all others, life is simple, natural, and only the present moment is inhabited. There is pain, but no suffering, an important distinction. Human beings win the honor of being the only living beings to drag themselves over the coals, replaying events of the past, and allowing a self-made inner critic to have any say whatsoever on these misremembered events. And some still believe humanity is superior, another idea made up in the mind.

The Zen Buddhist saying goes, "don't seek the truth; simply cease to cherish opinions." This is one of many profound statements whose full power was lost on this dense and survival-oriented mind, dismissing it as "nice, but couldn't possibly be *it*." Well, it is - in fact, this is the entire journey. Opinions, subjective ideas taken on based on the basic programming we took in during childhood and the experiences had since then, have all piled on top of one another, sometimes in conflict, and yet together they comprise much of the cause-and-effect computing machine we call the mind. They make up the smaller self, but actually do not reflect upon one's true identity at all. Of course, the ego is attached to the idea that our favorite band defines us in some way, that smoking will make us fit in with the edgy kids which will bring greater worth to our being, that being the oldest means we have to help others, that descending from an oppressed people means taking on the psychological and physiological burdens of that time for our entire lifetimes, as communicated to us by our guardians.

When we see others clinging to these ideas, and we have attained at least some level of discernment of the mind's content, we can see that if they would only drop these ideas, they could be free. And yet, when it comes to "me," it's not so simple. Why? Because your small self contains the ego - the limiting, judging, victim-identifying entity which seeks the continuation of its own existence. That ego isn't going to let go without a fight. "I *made* you," it says, "and if I die, so do you." This is why the simple act of dropping opinions, subjective and unverifiable beliefs which do not accurately reflect reality, can feel

## ONE THING AT A TIME

like life or death. I remember becoming quite upset when reading books in my early journey - "you don't understand what I'm up against, you haven't been [poor/ traumatized/ victimized/ neglected] like I have and the experiences aren't the same, I can feel myself falling apart!" My view of the situation required a slight recalibration - in fact, the *ego* felt threatened, felt it was falling apart, and the experience of my teacher matters not a fig so long as the lesson is completely sound and is allowed to resonate. And yet, ego sounded the alarm and carried on and on, keeping attention on it - so that the truth could be obscured for just a while longer. This ingenious evasive strategy is precisely how the collective has gotten into this situation in the first place - but don't worry. Help is coming.

Letting go of opinions, once you have overcome the initial pains of egoic aggression, is one of life's joys. To realize suddenly that you've been laboring under an idea which was never true leads to the instant realization that you are free - that all the energy spent in service of all the thoughts related to that belief is suddenly freed up. The only remaining obstacle, then, is attachment to life as is. Conditional acceptance you've received from loved ones may be revoked. Your friends may no longer spend time with you if you choose to spend your time or energy another way, no longer deriving an identity and a camaraderie from shared beliefs. Your partner may not appreciate your lack of interest in making enough money for luxury purchases, or they may not like it when you cease worshiping them, or you may notice friendships floundering when you no longer wish to gossip. An entire section of this book is dedicated to preparing for these experiences to unfold effortlessly and beautifully - a strong understanding of what you truly are will be sufficient in living in total peace and joy, come what may, attracting all manner of good things to you in support of your journey. It is also possible and common that some relationships will completely transform into healthier and happier ones, and you will know these as the "keepers," the ones meant to go forward with you. As new life circumstances take shape around you, it will be like wearing custom-made clothing after a lifetime of squeezing into the XL rubber glove the world told you was all you had to wear. As you ease into this, a newfound love will guide and protect you. In fact, you'll realize it was always there.

When you experience the arising of opinions, you will begin to question them. Byron Katie, a teacher who experienced spontaneous and continuous enlightenment in realizing that her thoughts were not true and that she was happier when she didn't believe them, calls her method "The Work" - in this work, she bids us to ask questions of our thoughts: are they true, can we prove it, how do we feel when we think them, and who would we be without them? Focusing only on the first question, in beginning to live life from a place of only true thoughts, all of the mind's delusions are systematically cleared at exactly the speed that we allow this to unfold. Later we will learn to inventory and scrutinize our way of thinking in a compassionate way. Under this scrutiny, you will quickly realize that you can trust virtually nobody to supply you with your beliefs, thoughts, and opinions - only you, with the fervent and earnest desire to realize what you truly are, will lead yourself to any sort of understanding about what that is. In the powerful paraphrased words of one of my teachers, S.N. Goenka, the founder of the international Vipassana meditation centers, "you are the only one who can work out your own liberation." Any expectation to the contrary comes from a subscription to concepts of life held in the mind - that others should help me, that if they don't I am entitled to upset and hurt and liable to fail or flounder, that I am entitled to create a victim identity from that upset and hurt. The idea that our salvation from suffering lies in some entity outside of us is one of the most limiting opinions and beliefs we can take on, and yet is almost completely pervasive in society. Imagine for a moment that within each human experience is the capability of liberating oneself from the misery of unchecked thought, and the only reason we have not done so is because of the belief that we cannot - this is the power of belief, of opinion. The releasing of opinions and views like these is precisely how the truth arises and fills every nook and cranny of newly opened space.

### Life is But A Dream

Imagine for a moment a self-correcting, self-learning program installed into a human body. This body, housing the program, walks the earth adding rules to its rulebook based on the things that happen and the other programmed people it encounters.

Now imagine that the creative spark and force of the universe is looking out through the eyes of this organic robot. This all-knowing non-thing has no need for speech or thought, as it knows its experience directly. This presence, capable of creating forms within a mind that it has constructed and of splitting itself into "pieces" capable of having distinct experiences, is enjoying *divine play* - Divinity itself, goofing around. It cannot see itself directly, because it has no attributes. It has created this world, which looks exactly the opposite of the consciousness that created it. Consciousness is peace and knowing, and yet it has created a world of chaos and ignorance; it, as the one timeless being, watches as the forms in the world are "born" into it and experience a life seemingly subject to time and gravity, which are built into the program. Each "individual" has the opportunity to sign up for the reality it will experience - and, as beliefs are taken on, this impacts the mind's way to navigating and narrating. As this forms, Consciousness experiences a vague feeling of loss, of separation from something it misses very much as there is indoctrination into thinking, and in relating to this thinking as a character, as "me" - and as such, these characters act out in various ways trying to find happiness - trying to find something about themselves they've lost. Some buy into the game of making themselves happy by possessing things, others try the game of deriving happiness from other living beings, and some begin to understand the rules of the game. They are working with minds which label experiences "pleasure" and "pain." Because in each experience there is the belief in oneself as separate, in identification with the mind, they have come to know pain as bad, they experience resistance to the pain via the mind, and so an even deeper layer of hurt called suffering is experienced. There is suffering because the attention of this powerful being has been absorbed, almost completely without ceasing, into the illusion, into the game, so that there is the experience of not knowing that all has always been well - in the illusion, they know only the game in which the human character is the star, and so this is what they see. The physics of this world are seamless, and they can't see around the illusion with the eyes and ears that the body is equipped with - the body was not designed to see past the illusion, but to navigate the game and reflect whatever the mind believes. And yet, somehow, the inner spark of clarity leads some of itself to find its way past all this through the miraculous process of recognizing that the apparatus through which they experience this dream game is not them - it is just a talking vehicle on loan for a time. Somehow, in dropping attachment to sensation and thought as the only information available, something else is gained, and that something is found to be everything.

As we learn to step back, allow yourself to imagine life loosely in this way, and eventually allow yourself to see what is without any filter or bias. You will realize this is no longer a mental exercise, but rather like the way things really are, and this just scratches the surface.

If you've ever wondered at the propensity of sentient beings to dream, you have touched on a big clue about the nature of reality. Each "piece" of Consciousness is like a co-dreamer of the universe, and ultimately "we" are all the one Dreamer. "We" will continue to be used throughout our time together, but it always refers ultimately to this one being that you are, that I am.

Each night that we dream, we buy into another reality for a time, even if that reality doesn't look like the waking one whatsoever. When we wake up, we wonder how we ever bought into it. It was so flimsy and there were clues everywhere! This is what it's like to awaken from the dream of earthly life - to realize that you have been living life staring at a virtual reality headset from day one, and you never thought to look at the screen for what it really is. You do not need to know the mechanics of the screen setup - in fact, trying to figure out how that works is a good way to get caught in the mind's activity for a while longer. You only need to be willing to consider that this dream movie is not everything, and suddenly you will begin to recognize the boundaries of the dream. Right now, when you really consider that your tendency to dream comes from the fact that deep within is The One Dreamer of the Universe, it makes intuitive sense that humans share a churning need to create, to use creative energy in constructive ways, and to constantly dream, in sleep and waking, of one's next creation. We can then see why so many are unhappy, having signed ourselves over to someone else's dream for us long ago and living within a society that seems to have robbed us of so much of our autonomy to create. In realizing this, insights flow in, we notice that our limitations are based on misunderstandings of the mind as well as our mistaken identification with the mind as "me," and as limitations are released, suddenly the seemingly impossible is occurring, like spontaneous healing or the ability to feel the internal energy and environment of the person next to you (wait - is "you" the you you think it is? Are you the one thinking of the mistaken you?"). We are still subject to the basic physics of the dream, but all extraneous and imagined limitations on those physics are removed as the mind releases them, which happens as we unsubscribe from the mind as "me." This is the true power of Consciousness via the mind when its brakes are taken off.

Most people spend their entire lives immersed in the dream, and once you begin to wake up, you will recognize the song and dance of daily life to be highly choreographed, with little room for a conscious and intentional will to be acted out. In its true meaning, karma is what comes about in our lives, partly based on what we came in with or the life circumstances that were unavoidable for this particular journey, and partly as a result of how much we are able to break from the choreographed dance within this lifetime to become truer and truer to ourselves. Rather than the reductive interpretation that karma is a kind of punishment system based on morality, understanding that it is actually a representation of the lessons we still need to learn based on how we are living is incredibly empowering.

Just as the idea that karma is attached to a moral system is not correct, the concept of sin is also not as we have come to understand it. In reality, both karma and sin refer to the degree to which one is true to themselves - to "sin against god" is to make life choices that are not in line with our authentic self, and will inevitably result in our being unhappy - living in "hell" is simply to be disconnected from the source of all love and understanding which is our true identity - life as it is for so many. To hurt others is to sin against the self, because we bring retribution, ill will, guilt, shame, or misrepresentative life circumstances upon ourselves and because that "other" is ultimately one and the same as "me." When we realize this as the basic structure of the dream world, we can drop all the erroneous concepts we've constructed around it - we can realize - make real to oneself - the state we call heaven, nirvana, samadhi, zen. We can also begin to understand why a world in which so many are attempting to secure their own happiness at the expense of others holds unprecedented despair.

### Doing Your Own Dance - Breaking the Cycle

Most people spend most of their lives acting out a fiction, which is why mental breakdowns and midlife crises exist within humans, but never in animals. Animals are honest, as they have no thoughts to confuse with their true self, and so no way to be socially conditioned against themselves and no propensity to do anything other than what they want to do. As such, they make excellent models for us as we are learning to break the cycle that we have been conditioned into - a cat will show you clearer than any human how to live life rent-free, shame-free, and effort-free while also drawing upon immense energy reserves when we so choose. When beginning the process of liberating this experience called Heather from its conditioned song and dance, the mind fixated on what seemed to be a great deal of resistance others showed at these changes, and I counted upon my cat, Luna, and many other creatures, to show me that although the humans I surrounded myself with at the time may (or may not) be nearly unanimous in their confusion over these new ways, all the pre-thought members of the animal world recognized these changes for what they were and had my back. Over time, I came to welcome signs that the small self had naturally done yet another deed which differed from the norm, as the mind was receding and allowing Consciousness to achieve what the mind used to unsuccessfully try to force through. Eventually, I found myself surrounded by the company I loved the most and recognized a community with those on a journey or in touch with their true nature. The dance of the higher Self is something which far surpasses the many missteps in trying to do a dance that was never meant for me - the new dance is easy, natural, and has brought more riches than the mind could dream of.

To break free from the cycle of suffering we find ourselves experiencing, we must come out of the hell of mistaken beliefs about life. There are multiple interpretations of best ways to do this. In Buddhism, the way is called the Eightfold Path - right living, thinking, and speaking which purifies the human body and mind unit until the higher Self can be heard. Yoga, which was being systematized around the same time that Gautama Buddha was realizing the true self through his own process, consists of the Eight Limbed Path - a similar process involving moral observances, physical cleansing and discipline, meditation, and use of the breath to work through the processes of the mind and body, arriving at a place where union, oneness, with the Divine is known continuously. While these paths will help guide ours, the beauty in this process is that we create our own.

### You Don't Have to Conquer The Mind

There is a common misconception amongst many seekers, students, and even teachers, that one must build up enough discipline within the bodymind to overcome thought - to one day stop it in its tracks. If you've tried meditating with this goal in mind, you've probably come out of it feeling worse than when you went in.

## ONE THING AT A TIME

Meditation is, in fact, meant to be an effortless process, but the ever-churning mind has commandeered the whole thing with the extraneous idea that becoming *good* at meditation takes *time*, and that mental calm comes only from years of suffering through daily sessions.

As with so much in the Universe, the truth is better than the mind thinks it is. There is no need to quiet the mind at all - trying to do this and becoming frustrated with a lack of results typically adds momentum to the mind, and is itself more mind activity being added to the constant feed. All that is needed is to recognize the truth about the contents of the mind: that thoughts are mostly wrong, mostly unnecessary, and definitely not you. The mind is a finite thing built for the finite world - it isn't meant for understanding the Infinite, and it's not going to. Read that again - the mind isn't going to understand the task you're shooting for, not in any person, ever. For those experiences in which the mystery of the Universe has been understood, this has been done so in a state that is beyond mind, beyond thought, and it has happened effortlessly at what might be called the soul level. This is why it is said that there is only one ultimate Truth in the Universe - when all the incorrect things the mind thinks are corrected or suspended, the outcome is always the same, with the world of form giving way to the deeper reality of Consciousness that we are - that I am. This is very important.

Instead of trying to calm the mind, when something comes up, we will learn to recognize it as mind activity - as small and unverifiable. When we do this, we begin to shift into the Infinite and verifiable. As you will soon find, almost no thing fits that description, and there is only one timeless message which is understood deeply by the one who has experienced this thoughtless peace: *I am the Infinite being, having an experience of the finite.* Said another way, *I am the Divine, having a human experience.* This is all one needs to know about life and the Universe in order to experience what is called enlightenment - but because the mind works overtime obscuring this one simple fact, we have endless talks, books, and exercises to move the mind beyond itself. If the mind could simply grasp this one statement, the rest of this book and any other book, talk, or retreat would not be written or undertaken. As the mind will obscure with all the energy and genius it has ever been fed, we seek teachers and pointers to continually help us recognize the mind has come up yet again. It is your choice from moment to moment - identify with the mind or with the Infinite.

Of course you don't seem like the Infinite - from the time you were two, the world has been shoving a virtual reality headset on your face and telling you *this* is the truth. You can't be upset with them, because they have headsets on too, and while more people are waking up today, there are still so many who do not know they have this headset on. You look and there is a body, you listen and there is a voice chattering on and on in the head - you come to believe it is your head, your voice, your body. Even as you read this book, it will keep being referred to as "your body" or "the body" because "the body you currently experience from this vantage point" is inconvenient. It really seems like it's you - not one human is at fault for buying into this game that infinite consciousness has created, as the intelligence behind it is beyond any the mind can understand, and in the end it is not the human who buys into anything, but the human who is bought into. The right words do not even exist to adequately describe the workings behind the game. To win, we simply realize we've been playing a game, peacefully opt out of the programming of the game, and directly experience our true nature. Of all the concepts, all the distractions and detours, this is really all there is to it. All else is taken care of.

**What You Believe is Your Reality**

The minds we are equipped with, however finite, have certain abilities - powers, if you will. The mind is a manifestation machine - what goes on within it consistently will eventually become part of this virtual reality. Other ways of saying this are "mind over matter," "if you can dream it, you can do it," and "energy flows where attention goes." If enough human experiences, powered by the attention placed on them, plug their mental power into a version of the game where nobody listens and it's hard to make friends, life circumstances are going to reflect that. If the collective consciousness representing humanity sways in the direction that this world is dangerous, it will appear so to those who currently conform to the majority, actions will follow, and reality will conform. To differ from the collective is difficult at first! This is why so few people are able to recognize on the practical level, "hey, I've actually lived 13,000 days on this planet and only on 20 or 100 of those days was this body in the kind of danger that warrants a fight-or-flight response, and here I still am fighting and flighting when I'm safe in my bed. I've spent all the remaining days fearing and feeling angry at danger out of habit, that fear itself has never once protected me, and I've noticed when I stop worrying happiness floods in. I can safely let this go."

I understand that if something truly traumatic has happened to your bodymind, which really seems like you, that bodymind has held onto that with an intention to keep itself safe. It is a vehicle for the Infinite, it has an important job! I spent years and years in total fear of other people, of heights, of living in a city because someone might be burning poison ivy in the next yard over at any moment, of living in the country because it's too far a drive to the nearest hospital. I understand that fear feels like life and death, anger feels completely essential to protecting yourself. However, as someone who has unsuccessfully medicated, meditated, and mediated until I finally sat and stared these "problems" in the face, I am here to tell you - they are nothing. They are processes in a mind which has no real physical location - the brain only shows the effects of the mind, the chemical reactions in the body caused by mind activity. A thought comes up, goes away, never even took up any physical space, and only remains if it continues to be brought up as memory. Recognize both the power and the flimsiness of thought and you change your life. True joy, the kind of joy which occurs when one is reunited with their true self (or in fact, when one realizes they never left themself), requires no cause, no thought. You do not need to be living in Hawai'i in a gated three bedroom two bathroom home with a mountain *and* ocean view. These things may be nice (or may not), but have nothing to do with the innate happiness lying just beneath the paltry objections of the mind. True and infinite happiness can descend upon you when you are in the middle of a divorce, without a job or a place to live (can confirm). When it happens, you will know without a doubt that it is something other than the mind, because you have lived with that binary machine for how long and not once has it been capable of this. The mind is a process created for the human apparatus to put structure to things - it has, over time, developed a few growths - collectively installed malware, if you will - which we call the ego and its aspects. The ego, in this context, is an entity designed and conditioned to act like and identify as a separate person, and subsequently fires off all sorts of processes to protect and amplify the identity it creates. This is not you. This is what you are watching unfold before you. You are watching a glorified calculator pretend to be you and to understand the immensity that you are.

Thoughts are nowhere. They can be watched, seen as false,

changed, and moved past. What matters is where attention is placed. For the duration of this bodymind, attention has been placed on the thoughts, on the constructed self. Now you move beyond the small creature, and your world opens up. What you allow to be true becomes true. In waking up one morning recently with a fear of all that is, only to watch it dissolve into nothing but an obvious series of constructed ideas which are simply false, leaving behind it a world of absolute potential and abundance - I tell you, your understanding can change that quickly. Allow for its possibility and it will.

### Opposites and Paradoxes

On this journey, there are several challenges. These challenges, when looked at properly, will become the substance that allows you to move past all limitation and into the Infinite. The first of these is the limitation of language. Language was constructed by the finite mind, and will never reach the Infinite. This baffled me for some time, but the more I looked at it, the more obvious it was - how could a mind built for limited functions ever understand its creator? How do you convince a three-year-old child they do not possess the vocabulary needed to explain complex ideas, when their mind cannot grasp that there are ideas it cannot grasp? The fact that humans think they are capable of infinite understanding using their finite tools alone is a likely outcome of the very egoic design of humanity itself.

In Christianity, Adam and Eve discovered the tree of the knowledge of good and evil. Not once in my childhood of regular churchgoing was this story explained to the point of my understanding it, seeming to be recited simply to describe the downfall of humanity, doomed and unworthy from the start. However, as with several pivotal passages in the Bible, when I came to understand them in context of Universal law and Truth, this resonated deeply as a metaphor for the arising of polarization within the human mind - there was the option to live in continuous and unconditional peace, but the idea was adopted that some things in life are good and some are bad or evil, with our own exposed bodies topping the list of evils at the time, because what else was there. This view is ever-so-slightly different from the classic one - the problem isn't evil, it's the *idea* of evil and the fact that once it is conceived of, reality begins to resemble this concept, with humans outright perpetuating it with their own minds and actions. In other words, the only problem is that we think there's a problem. Even more accurate -

the only problem is that I identify with and believe the entity playing out a drama of problems. In this, we place conditions upon the ability to be happy with this earthly experience, and this is to strongly sin against our true Self, who delights in all things and has already deemed everything under the sun to be good. This deviation became the basis for suffering, as these binary minds changed our perspective of the very surroundings we experienced. The Buddha's Four Noble Truths tell us the same thing - that in life there is suffering, that suffering comes from attachment to life going a certain way, and the way out is through relinquishing of attachment to these concepts of good and bad to allow the outward experience to reflect the peace that comes from our true nature, of unconditional happiness with what is. The common threads which are so seamlessly tying all the major religions and philosophies together, all ultimately pointing to the same thing, are one of life's beautiful and illuminating ironies.

When we understand that the true self is actually akin to that force which holds the world together, we understand that to sin is to go against what is harmonious in us. It never referred to a code of morality. Despite a dogmatic upbringing, as I experience softening and coming to understand what aligns with the real me, nowhere in that list of things is the chastising over what others might deem shortcomings. In the days of the symbolic Adam and Eve, there were no requirements upon humanity - no jobs, no morality; only a life to be enjoyed effortlessly. Nobody told them they must have a function or an outer sense of purpose beyond enjoying a body created just to traverse a splendid and bountiful earth. While today you may choose to have a job to avoid the apparent displeasure of not adhering to the procedures and systems humans have erroneously established, the idea that we should derive self-worth from our ability to function in this nonsensical structure is completely mistaken. Humans are here to facilitate the exploration of form to allow a better view of that which is not form, end of story. As one who has experienced a character in existential dread in performing the busy work of pushing around others' money, in frustration at "healing" those who continually injure themselves, and in resistance to the task of fitting into society, until all ideas of being humanly "good" at this were released and play was pursued rather than work - being good at work ain't it. It is one possible outcome in an entire vast universe of forms. The one thing we are trying to be good at is one large distraction from that which truly is.

Right, wrong, good, and bad are human constructs. These constructs give the ego the opportunity to draw lines and find fault in the weather, the temperature of bathwater, and the taste of food which they did not toil to grow or prepare. This is where opinions originate. The release of all notion of good and bad is the healing of the Adam and Eve Problem - the fundamental veering-off-path of humanity. The release of these polarizing ideas also releases the word "should" - the idea that life is better when it goes in a particular direction. If this sounds easy to release, I'm nobody to tell you otherwise, go for it! But if you find that trying to release these ideas exposes you to a world of hurt you never knew was there and you don't know where to begin, you're in good company. Together, we will make lists, and these lists will help, as long as we are also prepared to throw these lists away.

When a child is reared in a binary environment, it can be very difficult to make decisions as an adult. Instead of pursuing that which is most natural to us, we follow the supposed flow of society, trying not to rock some invisible and ever-present boat. This is the silent desperation which Henry David Thoreau spoke of - the one thing that tamps down the naturally loving and flowing spirit. The good news is, you do not require others in this dream to be liberated from their suffering in order to experience this ease and flow. Your liberation will be contagious to those experiences within which there is readiness to see, but does not require others to do anything for it to exist. It requires you to drop polarity and embrace the ultimate positive impartiality that is equanimity - a gentle happiness and openness to whatever unfolds in a given moment. In this, balance returns to the bodymind, and life is ease and joy. This is a real thing that you can experience in this lifetime. You are the Creator of the Universe dressed in a skinsuit - in fact, in many many human skinsuits, and treesuits, and catsuits - that is in no way hyperbolic or fanciful, so really take it in - and you are here to create your world how you see fit.

### Getting Lost in the Journey

The journey to the self can sometimes become a distraction of its own. Even the word journey is a sign pointing you in the wrong direction if taken too literally, because there is no need to go anywhere to find what you are looking for. You, the infinite being, chose to experience a human body, and from a young age in that body, others began to tell you your limitations and values. Some part of you knows that you are Infinite, but all is being experienced through the filter of the mind, seemingly obscuring the truth, and definitely distracting your attention so much that it cannot rest on the truth for more than a rare moment. In true poetic beauty, the very unhappiness you witness as a result of having bought into mistruths about life is the experience that you will use to find your way back, and as you know, you don't need to go to a retreat on a remote island to notice your own unhappiness. To go within, to observe the beliefs leading to unhappiness with complete willingness to let them and everything else go, is enough to realize the true Self completely and live in joy. Gautama Buddha, a regular mortal man with a great deal of suffering upon seeing the suffering of humanity outside his sheltered life, went on a great journey which led him no closer to enlightenment until one day inspiration and strong will arose, leading him to sit with reality until the truth was understood. Within himself, with no outside interference, the self was realized. It was realized that this body hailing from clan Gautama was not solid - that all solidity fell away under the light of Consciousness, and that Consciousness was his true identity. That is, when he looked with an open mind at what was truly being experienced, it became completely obvious to him (truly, to the Consciousness powering the experience) that the body was not solid, that Consciousness was not tied to the body, that all belief was obscuring Truth, that universal Truth was comprised of only one fact, and yet there were many ways to talk around and in the direction of it, which he would spend the rest of his life doing effortlessly.

Anyone can be a Buddha, a word and title which means "enlightened one." It seems a distraction that humanity has collectively attributed this title in such an exclusive way to the man who systematized a way of realizing the self, because it appears as though he was somehow superior to other humans. In fact, there had been great suffering as well as sheltering from the outside world, and circumstances collided to produce in that experience a strong determination to move past it - the only requirement for realizing the true Self. To recognize Buddha Consciousness as the very same Consciousness that you are, simply having an experience from a different perspective, is to drop the walls to attainment of this understanding.

You can spend thousands of dollars to be in the presence of a teacher you revere or fellow "seekers." You can gain an intellectual understanding of complex spiritual ideas and seek after interesting experiences within the body. You can make a successful profession out of helping others, or do it for free. You can play the same audiobook on repeat for months to experience immersion of new ideas which create resonance within. All of these things *may* contribute to the ultimate understanding of who you are, but they will not directly bring you to it. Often through trial and error we are able to see what does not work and eventually there is enough understanding to realize the mind just doesn't know - this results in surrender, which makes way for the ultimate knowing. This is fine. But know this: you do not need to go anywhere or do anything to realize the truth. It is right in front of you, within you, you yourself, waiting to be seen. Many times I have heard this and practically snorted with derision at what was perceived to be yet another teacher oversimplifying things, but I tell you, it is true. You must simply be open and willing enough. In Chapter Nine, we will look at several exercises which will help prepare your experience to go beyond reliance on the mind - and yet, in a world where humans were not exchanging mistruths left and right from day one, these exercises would not be necessary. You are the key, and you will determine how long the journey will carry on. And while in this particular phase of life on earth awakening is becoming more and more accessible to even more people, if only an intermittent awakening occurs within this lifetime, remember: there is no shame, blame, agenda, or problem in that. What happens in this game is of little consequence to who you really are, and underneath it all, as we will discuss, it's all okay.

 I spent seventeen years seeking the truth, and after all those years, while mind had become less judgmental of itself and gained some surface-level understanding of what it was to let go, I still experienced conflict in interpersonal relationships and was unconsciously expending all my life energy trying to attain a place of distinction among society - trying very hard to appear a certain way. This is extremely common even or especially in spiritual teachers, and even when they approach their work from a genuine desire to help others. When the trying stops, effortlessness and all that flows from it are experienced. Knowing this, I will never intentionally try again.

 Knowing that the ego is constantly trying to distinguish itself, it is easy to make an enemy of it - to become angry at it. But this is really the ego becoming angry with the ego while creating yet another effective distraction - using the anger to add fuel to itself, as it feeds on feelings of otherness, anger, and separation. This is what it is! And yet, it has a quality of innocence - of not really knowing what it is doing. Ego is separate from Consciousness, a mechanism of the game I'm playing with specific programmed parameters. Identifying this innocence in the ego, and in the ego of other humans, you can easily see that everyone is just trying to be happy and we're all attempting it with equipment that has been programmed against happiness. Those who lash out at others are trying to create some kind of parallel of their inner state - we don't want to be alone in our suffering. Recognizing attempts to create "others", villains, in our story and realizing our own inner innocent villain-maker, we move past it. In this, we create a new world based on our updated understanding - one without limitations, without villains. In this, our journey will be brief and direct, allowing unimpeded experience of the happiness that exists within the true Self.

# CHAPTER TWO

## UNLEARNING FROM UNTEACHERS

A wonderful place to start one's journey is in recognizing what no longer works in their life. I want to be very clear here: this is not the ultimate truth of who you really are. This is a tangible exercise to begin to see through the web of mind, to use the mind to deconstruct itself to the point that insight can be recognized and resonated with.

It may help to create a written inventory, especially as at this point the mind might be rather chaotic and require some structure or accountability. We will get into this further in Chapter Nine, but for now, begin to pay attention to your life circumstances and thoughts. Take a good look and ask, *what no longer works for me?* We can break this list down further into these questions:

What are the values, beliefs, and habitual reactions of my constructed self?
Where did I learn all of these things?
Are the people who instilled and modeled these beliefs, values, and reactions genuinely happy most to all of the time?
Did I willingly consent to a world based on these constructs, or were they told to me until I bought them?

It might be challenging at first to identify beliefs, values, and reactions, so let's work through some commonly held ones to jog the memory. Most humans come into this world as part of a family which holds some sort of religious or philosophical belief, and perhaps a sense of their nationality, from which they derive a sense of identity.

"The MacClarens have a strong history in Scotland, we are a well-respected family. Even in the U.S., people know this. You will need to behave in a way that reflects positively on us." "We all drink and laugh together as a family, anyone who doesn't is uptight, unless they're in recovery." "We don't air our dirty laundry." "We don't go to the doctor in this family." "We don't call the police, we take care of it ourselves." "The daughters of this family are not expected to work, but should make a good match during high school or college." All of these are beliefs and values which are completely irrelevant, unverifiable, and flimsy in the scheme of the world, and yet could cause one individual who seeks to equally co-create this world loads of havoc if bought into. If that individual is able to recognize that their family is simply recirculating someone else's ideas from a fear of veering off course, and that individual has done the work to determine what they will choose to take on, it will cause them no suffering whatsoever when their family chooses to become upset at their living authentically. However, if the individual buys into these beliefs, which cannot possibly represent Universal Truth and in every way limit the limitless to being only one small person, they are the power of the Universe acting like a tiny pointless pinpoint. This will lead to unhappiness and a sense that something was lost along the way.

If there is still difficulty in identifying the beliefs and values internalized throughout your life, this is a good time to begin talking back to the mind. Set an intention to become aware of the inner voice, and follow it up with time set aside, maybe with a pen and paper handy. Then, notice all the opinions voiced throughout a given day - "that skirt is too short" is an opinion which opens us to our deeper beliefs - that our opinion of another's clothing even needs to exist, that this opinion somehow holds some kind of validity, that the way others live their lives is subject to scrutiny even when it is not harming another. Minds are a trove of cursed treasure when it comes to opinions and beliefs, and soon after you ask to be shown, you will see.

Once you have a list prepared, this is a good starting point for your journey. Releasing false beliefs, values, and reactions will be a helpful place to start when recognizing what we have to unlearn, and who our "unteachers" - those people or situations who have laid the foundation of our path by showing us what leads to unhappiness and where our work lies - are.

### Messengers

Another way of looking at the "work" ahead of you, and the material you have brought with you to be worked through, is through the identification of messengers. Messengers are the root causes of our negative feelings, and I like to think of them as the built-in alarms that tell us when we are off track in our lives, showing us the seed of any discomfort and acquired dis-ease in us. Take a mental inventory of the challenges you currently face in your life. Examples: *I want to start a business but am too afraid, I can't finish my book, my friends are disrespectful and I am too afraid to talk to them about it or make new friends, I can't stop acquiring or wanting to acquire new or expensive things.* Now, for each of these challenges, take a look at how you feel when you think about them - where are your "shoulds?" For each obstacle, consider what belief is behind this negative feeling. Below are just a few ways of categorizing these, which were given to me by my teacher, Michelle Young, owner of My Vinyasa Practice yoga school.

Limited - not enough capacity, energy, etc.

Time-bound - too old, running out of time, too young, etc.

Lacking - don't have what other people have, or what I should have

Confused or disconnected - lack of clarity and connection to surroundings

Incomplete - needing to achieve or acquire something in order to earn your place on earth

Remember, as our true identity which is the one Divine being breathing life into and conceiving of all things, we are limitless, timeless, whole, complete, clear, and connected. We come into this world with clean slates, and we learn all limitations from the humans around us. All human vessels are cooperating in a joint venture, participating in an ongoing illusion, and all bodies are powered by Consciousness, all participation is subject to the consent of Consciousness to play these parts. Anything that makes us feel other than what we are at our core is part of the vast web of human conditioning, humans are the only ones on earth subjecting themselves to this, they created it, and they do not need it in their lives; the game can be played another way if desired. Unlearning some of these ideas from our unteachers can make waves and feel difficult at first, but ultimately allows us to go beyond the turbulent surface to the calm and unchanging ocean beneath. So, if I hang around friends who don't appreciate me and I am afraid to speak up, what is it that has made me believe I should be quiet, that unhappiness is my lot in life or is better than experiencing another person possibly becoming upset by their own perceptions of my words? The belief that I am less than, incomplete, and limited. When did I learn this? Look around and take your pick, focusing on the particularly strong memories. If you have specific unteachers in each case, make note of them. Now comes the two part solution - correction and forgiveness. Recognizing that these beliefs are false, that the promoters of this false information know no better themselves, that they too suffer as a result, and that this suffering is perpetual and collective over the history of humanity, suddenly it is seen clearly - humans are unaware of the harm they inflict because they don't understand where suffering comes from - the mind churning out resentful thoughts cannot fathom the total and beautiful interconnectedness of every character in this game. This is an important point that we will revisit later. To realize the vastness of human unconsciousness is to begin to understand you've simply been playing a part in a Divine play until now. Recognize that until this point you have also been largely unconscious. Forgive yourself for buying into the idea that you are anything less than whole and complete - after all, it's a nearly seamless illusion until you look for the seams. Since society has collectively established the idea that our own happiness depends upon others, you can forgive others for buying into their own incompleteness as well as yours. We can only speak and act based on our level of understanding of what is really true.

I learned this concept as part of a coaching program based on the tenets of mindfulness. This presentation is just a new way of saying an old thing: attachment to our thoughts, as we have come to use and experience them, is in the way of a clean experience of life in a human body on Earth. In the context in which I learned it, this coaching structure is designed to help people go past their self-imposed limitations with the overall intention of goal attainment. I had no idea when I studied this material that within it was the heart of self-realization - what I would eventually come to understand as the only universal Truth. That you are whole, complete, and Divine is the only thing you need to know to be endlessly, causelessly happy. I spent decades in the perspective of "no that's wrong, I can't be happy with [present circumstance], your life has allowed you to be happy and mine hasn't." I can now tell you unflinchingly this is just another quite changeable machination of the ego, and that thought is the only thing in the way of happiness, because during the "worst" time of my life, after so much suffering that the mind was ready to relent, I became willing to see absolutely everything in the world differently, and my experience of the entire world shifted, suddenly seeing it for what it was. Nothing in my circumstances had changed, yet all was new.

A note on forgiveness, to be repeated: this is an exercise for the constructed self. The purpose of this is to release negative energy in the body, as well as its source. This is, overall, prep work. When practiced consistently, it creates space for understanding, capacity to open to what differs with an existing worldview. However, in the end, we will realize nothing ever needed to be forgiven.

Despite the fact that there is only one truth which becomes realized as soon as we drop all the extraneous beliefs and mental clutter we've accumulated, a great deal of resistance may still be present even after you have gained a surface-level realization of the truth, and the mind may have built up an obstacle course it will seemingly need to run to get past its own nonsense - the only reason why this book is more than two chapters, why there are so many teachers and traditions pointing in different ways to the same thing. The truth is so simple, and yet the mind proves a formidable veil.

### A Blessing and a Curse

It took almost two decades of practice, vacillating between intermittent and consistent, to realize that the things which present challenges as the character I'd invented were exactly the things that would lead to self-realization. I thought of this as a rather mystical and cryptic way of looking at things until one day, it became a literal reality for me. It suddenly clicked into place that the only way to realize the Divinity powering the humanity that we are experiencing is through the nagging complaints within the bodymind - the things that spur us to seek a solution to this feeling that seems it "shouldn't" be there. Without supposed problems, there would be no reason to ask any questions, and nothing to form the contrast which helps us to recognize what we seek when we find it. I can certainly attest that my younger self, not having suffered enough, lacked empathy, perspective, and a sufficient reason to seek. I had not yet knowingly and directly experienced fear of death and had grown up feeling rather insulated and safe, so mind could not understand the humans around me acting in erratic ways trying to assuage the feelings of emptiness and unsafety. Once I had gained some perspective through suffering, mind wanted to fix people because there was believing and fancying myself capable of doing that, as well as craving gratification. There was an underlying belief that the human character could do anything at all by itself, that prevented me from asking the important questions. When people would say, "we are just a product of our environment," mind would pridefully think, *not me! I've built myself from the ground up. My self.* Through death of loved ones, divorce, illness, rejection, and the absolute pummeling experienced as a result of my insistence upon trying to act like a small human being, it is as though the small self has had no choice in the matter - the more egoic that character called "me" was, the more the thoughts and choices led to suffering, which led to teachers and timing, which led to the right messages hitting the right way. Consciousness is showing itself to itself through the myriad seemingly chaotic and pointless happenings of each day.

In understanding this, we can also begin to see that bad feelings in the body are excellent messengers - matched only by the emergence of positive feelings which we come to recognize were there all this time, being seemingly stifled and covered over by an entity other than our true identity. The resistance of the mind often manifests itself as hardness, heat, and tenderness in the body - in other words, discomfort and eventually dis-ease. The fact that humanity now experiences unprecedented numbers of self-caused dis-ease, which we often chalk up to "stress and environmental factors" as though there is no choice in the matter, is evidence both of unconsciousness and of the ripeness of the moment for awakening to occur. I do not say this from the perspective of someone who has maintained perfect health and seen "others" fall ill - this is from the direct experience of falling ill each time I have undergone something I deem traumatic, realizing that I've deemed it traumatic because of my training as a human, then deciding to see it otherwise, and watching symptoms vanish and give way to unimaginable relief and joy, as well as seeing this in many patients and friends willing to do that work. That which has seemed to hurt the character we are playing has become our reason for seeking, for finally being willing to surrender that which has so clearly led us astray. We begin to understand that psychosomatic pain in the body is the body working exactly as it should, like a car dashboard. The body alerting us to a problem that can be solved simply by realizing attention has once again been absorbed in the mind is the beginning of using that which seems to hurt us for our own benefit. Through the understanding of how these emotions generally show up in the body, which we will get into shortly, we can become quite precise in our self-healing and much more direct on our so-called path to realization of the Truth.

**All The World's A Stage**

"All the world's a stage, and all the men and women merely players. They have their exits and their entrances; and one man in his time plays many parts." Shakespeare's famous line is all the more poignant when we deeply consider it to be literally true. When we look at the roles we have taken on, tweaked, and dropped within a lifetime, which of those was truly "me"? As a child, my mother was very busy, and it was hard to get her attention. I demanded her attention because from a young age I had been conditioned to believe in "good" and "bad" like most other children, and I had a strong desire to be "good." Life was showing me that to be "good," one must continually be called that; must impress and delight others. This is engrained so deeply as to seem connected to our very survival, and so, despite the fact that it brings almost constant tension and misery even in childhood, we take on this task. As obvious as this might sound, it is likely that most people you know are caught in this web without really understanding it on a deeper level.

As a pre-teen on family vacation, we went swimming in the pool at our relative's home. By this time I was highly insecure, and ever in need of validation, I swam back and forth, showing the adults how quickly I could swim. One adult took note, visibly impressed, and told me I should join the swim team. Not long after that, I was enrolled in the swim program with the YMCA, my guardians driving me over a half hour to practice a few nights a week after work and school. This began to snowball, as I didn't understand why I would go through so much work at practice not to compete in all the competitive team swim meets, but my mother informed me she only had so much time and money to invest in this. Rather than enjoying my family's ability to pay for and support my ability to swim indoors all winter long, I wanted accolades, proof that I could show to others, via stressful matches and harder practices. I had turned a simple pleasure into an egoic way to gain distinction in the world, and I had managed this at the age of twelve. Continuing these tendencies into adulthood, we can see how the personal selves are but players on the stage of life, adopting values and beliefs from those who talk loudest.

## We Are the Children

The best way to understand unconsciousness without making it into an enemy is to observe children over the age of three. These little balls of love, operating with half-formed versions of the finite equipment we call the bodymind, open to the reality of their full powers but experiencing amnesia and brainwashing, and absolutely enraged at being treated as anything other than whole, complete, and autonomous, are grappling with a loss of all that brings them endless joy. Introduction on this planet is not a gentle one - *read this, say this, don't do this, act your age, stop crying or I'll give you a reason to cry* - adults have been parenting at this level for as long as we have called ourselves civilized. Since humans are on earth to enable the experience of the finite and changing, we assume the roles - but we miss something we never knew we had. In order to function in this society, children must have an identity, a name - that name will come to be associated with certain traits in itself and in association with our personal deeds. Today is a phenomenal time to see the way one can be judged based on their name alone - Karens the world over are deemed crotchety - Kimberly is thought to have limited intelligence - Krystal comes from the wrong side of town - Brad is a dime a dozen, and probably a jerk. To what extent are we identifying with this one arbitrary label? Coming into such a world, children are rightfully confused - *excuse me, I was under the impression I was going to be able to do what I wanted? I mean, I'm the force that holds the Universe together and the creator of this experience!* Carry this into adulthood, and you can see why our attempts to make ourselves happy are so miscalibrated - we are following the values of others when we could be following the all-knowing always-right inner Knowing that the characters we've invented and the equipment we are using don't even know is there.

Understanding the deeper meaning of innocence, we can begin to see how a bundle of joy can hit, scream, and raise trouble. In innocence, there is a curiosity about life - just as a cat can play with its food before killing it, a child may take a magnifying glass to an ant - there is no malice, unless it has already been modeled strongly for them and they are acting it out to try to release some of that energy, and yet a needless destruction can occur. This is a natural form that nature takes, just as an ocean wave can delight or drown, the sun can nourish and scorch. In this, removing the concept of good and bad from a thing, we begin to understand what it is to live with equanimity - an understanding of the Universe as a neutral thing that is what it is - an impartial welcoming of all things. Innocence, tempered with equanimity, is to welcome all experiences without any learned traits of fear, morality, or resentment.

Applying understanding of this process to life situations, all conflict ceases - the conscious aspect of any human experience is the same, a filtered bit of the same soul-like non-thing, seeming to have journeyed away from itself and looking for the way back, which is right here and now, to ultimate peace and love with greater understanding of itself. Consciousness is playing the game of form until it's done, and in that game, I, Consciousness itself, am having the experience of not remembering that I am the Infinite. The finite mask, the bodymind, thinks I am small, vulnerable, bound to be hurt and eventually to no longer exist. The very nature of the mind is finite and subject to delusion - that does not render it bad. It simply is. Of course that self is going to behave erratically. To recognize this unconsciousness all around you and still to pursue the path of self-realization is not something that the smaller self can be applauded for - once again, the higher self, Consciousness, is showing itself to itself, and all that must be done is to drop resistance to what is occurring in each moment, to experience it fully without commentary. To fervently pursue the path to self-realization is to heed the glimmer of Divine Will still being heard above the mind's goings-on. To realize there is no path is to grasp the Truth.

**Putting Labels on the Unlabellable**

When you realize that you have created a character that is ultimately a combination of parents, siblings, friends, teachers, and maybe even people you don't know, it can be an incredibly vulnerable moment. Many of us walk the earth seeing ourselves as a failure, a success, a victim, a villain - in reality, most humans are reflective of each of these traits at different times and even in one day, yet these words are so far from defining you. Even as the constructed self, how could we be defined by just one trait, and how can we identify with one when we contain its opposite? When you begin to notice yourself gossiping, talking down about yourself just to get laughs, or judging the most minute of traits in others, eventually you will have the realization that the small self is hurting itself in this moment, and you are experiencing it via the human apparatus. If all beings are co-creators in the world of form, what this mind is currently contributing to that world is not constructive. It is deconstructing or judging creation, and that is not the nature of the Divine. As phrased by Christians, God looked upon all of creation and said that it was good - when we are acting as the Divinity that we are (here referred to not as a previously formed idea of God but as the one thing which cannot be described, and our true identity), we will see all as good. Looking at this deeper, when finding fault with creation, you are "sinning" in the original and true meaning of the word - you are putting out that which hurts you, because the boundary between "this" form and "other" forms is not really there, yet the mind is perpetuating it. In the world of form, each of these apparently separate bodies is housing one sliver of the same Consciousness - the one who beats the hearts and breathes the lungs of all other beings beats your heart and breathes your lungs - in fact, they are not any more yours than the other ones. This is in no way metaphorical or spiritual - this is the reality that all sages have come to realize.

In realizing that you have internalized the labels your friends and parents placed on you as a child, and that you as the Infinite are so incredibly autonomous that it is laughable that you are carrying around these ideas as limitations, you will realize the prison you have imagined yourself to inhabit is actually a collection of chains you willingly grip onto and lug around in this dream world. Every time we block our view of the sky in the name of commerce, choose financial stress over ease for the sake of an outer appearance, or ignore the low-maintenance, loving friend in favor of the flashy one who we must chase, we have agreed to a way of living and a set of values that comes with experiences, which affects our thoughts, which affects our emotions and our energy level daily. We look for happiness rather than realizing we are it, so we needlessly spend our resources. We are only capable of doing this when we have forgotten our true nature - and as society stands, that is the present reality within most human experiences.

The idea of being "strong" becomes absurd when you realize that you are the Consciousness that creates all things, the space-like thing in which they appear. The idea of being good or bad, or of being good looking or successful, is completely irrelevant except to notice the experience of that on earth and contrast it with the unconditional love that one truly is. The idea of being moral from obligation, especially when it conflicts with true inspiration and intuition, makes no sense when you realize you are the creator of all things and your nature is to continue to create how you see fit. All outside the basic process of creation and experience is a hindrance to that - having the experience of feeling bad is having veered off of true understanding.

**Shoulda Woulda**
The most impactful habit you can begin to unlearn is that of attachment. In fact, in wanting life to go a certain way, you subject yourself to the one cause of suffering. That's right - Gautama Buddha, Jesus, Lao Tzu, and the many great sages of times past and present agree - wanting life to go our way is precisely the thing that prevents us from being happy. It sounds rather absurd when I say it that way, doesn't it - "I'm not going to be happy until things go my way" sounds like a toddler losing their cool over apple juice versus orange juice - just enjoy the juice! Just feel the coolness on the tongue, the sweetness, enjoy the sensation as it is swallowed and travels down the throat until you lose sensation of it. Savor every sip! When you admit that you've been waiting for various elements outside of your control to align before you'll be happy, and that even when all manages to align with your wants you'll suspend that happiness again when you think of something else you want, you'll know without a doubt your whole idea of happiness is wrong. If, however, you would choose to simply be happy, because it feels good, because it is easy, because it is right there for the choosing, your life would be transformed with the one action. Why can't you just choose to be happy? Because you have been told from the beginning that somehow to not be successful, to not have children, to not be married, to not graduate from college, to not be a doctor or an entrepreneur or an electrician like your easily disappointed parental figure, are things that should elicit an unhappy response and will cause you ongoing unhappiness until these things are achieved. You have also seen that when they are achieved, a brief happiness is experienced before a new goal is set. Whether it makes sense or not, the mind has absorbed this mode of being for its own survival - to fit in. Your mind is churning out unhappy thoughts because it is trained to do it, and you eventually folded to the collective will of your trainers. In believing this is how it will go, you've authorized the mind to function based on this parameter.

## ONE THING AT A TIME

In realizing that you are not the mind, that the mind is putting on a play and you are watching that play, happiness and relief overtake you. Suddenly, you have no investment in doing what others are doing - you also don't need to go out and blaze your own trail with a vengeance. In fact, you don't need to do anything at all. When I have felt the habitual pangs of unfulfillment as I have tried in vain to rest and only felt guilt at not working, or when my life was not where it seemed it should be, I would often remind myself of the well-known figures in India, sitting in the same place day after day meditating, perhaps only eating when kind passersby would put food into their mouths. They appear to be neither successful, nor productive, nor fitting into the supposed flow of society, and yet they are perfectly acceptable where they are. The simple adjustment of birth circumstances would make this way of life completely acceptable in my surroundings, this is how arbitrary the moral and ethical code is. But deeper than that, I recognize that the character is still comparing itself to other human beings as some frame of reference. It does not matter to the Infinite being that I truly am.

You are meant to let go of any single thing the world has told you to be - there is not one correct way in all the world, and there is no human-made hierarchy of any kind in the realm of the formless, timeless Infinite that is the entire basis of all this. Effortlessness is the ultimate honoring and embodiment of one's true nature.

# CHAPTER THREE

## THE "OTHER"

A great misunderstanding has been perpetuated about the dream world being experienced. This is that I am an individual, a human being - that everything else is the "other." We believe that because we can see supposed borders to forms that they, that we, must ultimately be separate. Similarly, we cannot see or detect a connection between forms using our senses. Then, when physics tells us that all this energy is one thing, we don't make the connection "this must mean I can't just be the one human," because we already heavily buy into this and it makes all the appearances look completely real and solid. As for detecting that which unites all things, we are talking about the ultimate intangible non-entity which is not of the world of form - it is not going to be seen by the eyes that are a part of a tangible and finite form, and certainly won't be seen by the instruments conceived of these finite minds. This is the greatest mystery of life - something that every being (really just little packages of Consciousness, which are not separate or plural in the end) can experience if we choose to - and yet, if we choose not to, we will never catch even one glimpse.

Once we take in the idea that we are a separate being in early childhood, we rail against many things. We want, we need, we demand, we rebel - we have already started trying to fill the hole left by lacking the understanding that we are whole and complete, now seemingly lost to us in this filtered reality. This little entity we call an identity is bolstered and fueled throughout childhood and into adulthood, where we witness egos butting up against each other unceasingly. These egos say, "mine! You bad. Me good. Me bad? Me mad!"

Part of the creation of this ego is to begin to deem other forms as separate - the "other." We begin to want the best things for ourselves, and for others to have just a little less than us. Many egos struggle with seeing others happy. Many egos cannot even bear to listen to another's story without immediately interjecting, "well me too, but better!"

The ego, with its programmed tendency to live life as a separate being, has a vested interest in furthering itself, and in furthering the narrative that all the world is separate from "me." In encountering the Divine that I am, simply wearing the various disguises of other human beings, the mind says, "ugly dress, jerky smirk, I wouldn't do it that way, that one looks nice, I want that one to like me, I want to feel ownership over that one." And when this happens, the body shows it; the heart will begin to contract, a sign of fear and separation.

One way humans attempt to solidify their identities is by joining groups which will give a heightened sense of belonging based on the ideas that have been selected to take in from our surroundings. Mind thinks, "this is me," and our attention is completely absorbed in this, when really, we are just watching a character in a movie, and the script says we join groups based on outward traits that appeal to the character, until we realize what we are doing. This character says, "my beliefs are the truth, and I believe this on faith. My friends are better than yours. My friends are more righteous, more liberated, tougher, more badass, more musically inclined, on the right side of history." The next time you find yourself feeling pride about a group you belong to or associate with, or even a personal pride or lamentation over how much of a loner you are, investigate this feeling. Where is it felt in the body? Is there another aspect of your experience that indicates disagreement, resistance, tension, or would rather just not be sure? Even when you feel pride, can you feel a nagging insecurity beneath it saying, "I want this feeling to stay, I want this to be who I am" or "all the excitement of being around my friends makes me tired"?

I like to see every one of these identity-based thoughts like a calorie burned - energy I started the day with that is with me no more, because of the choice to spend it to maintain a personality that cannot make its mind up to save the world. And if you think your personality is completely decided, energy is also expended in that, in the constant resisting of whatever differs from it.

There is also a sense of each thought as resulting in a signal sent in the brain, every single thought becoming a chemical reaction. In this way, it is easy to understand how our very bodies are formed by our thoughts - tight, hard, exclusive thinking results in a body, which is ultimately just energy doing what we tell it to, that reflects those thoughts - aches, pains, constricted nerves and blood vessels. Practitioners of Ayurveda, Traditional Chinese Medicine, modern alternative healing modalities, and even some Western medical practitioners are aware that our bodies are cooperative systems, and the mind is a layer of that system completely overlaid on all physical parts of it. When we "other" people, we feel the effects of it. The beauty of this path is that you do not need to buy into anything proclaimed by a group you don't feel you identify with - you don't need to buy into the words of ancient texts or even this one, but rather you must strike the balance between openness to them and higher discernment based on actual experiences - when you do that, you begin to notice the entirety of the experience within the body without any skew or filter, and you will notice that when you give away your power, you feel it; when you believe false thoughts, it reflects in the body; everything bought into becomes something physical in the vessel seeming to carry you around. After years of progressively deeper observation, I have learned to use the inborn ability to affect my body, as in noticing a headache and recognizing the tense thoughts causing the body to contract, allowing the muscles to release on command. Because of this I can know, rather than believe, that what I think, or even more accurately, what I choose to believe from the mind's thoughts, becomes my most direct reality. On your journey, you can begin to teach yourself the very same as you learn to experience directly, and yet even this is a kind of subplot in the story.

**The Word and Collective Creation**

In his book "The Four Agreements," Don Miguel Ruiz describes the dream of the planet - the world of form that is being co-created in real time with every action, every thought that is conceived in the mind and acted out by humans. In this world of form, our word is our ultimate power - through thoughts and speech, we are creating.

In this dream creation, according to Ruiz and Toltec wisdom, when we use the power of our word to gossip, to spread a negative opinion, to create division, or to harm, we are taking part in the creation of a dream of hell. When you put out bad against someone else, you are sinning against yourself, because you are inviting negative energy to return to you. Taking it a step further, when we realize that the same energy is being vibrated into the appearance of different bodies, we see that energy is being influenced to work against the very same energy, and it's all being experienced by one being - you, me, us, I.

This is an extremely helpful way to view the world of form. However, this was yet another book I read many years ago which I did not grasp as the truth - only a poetic and flowery way of describing the world, according to a hardened Western mind. I have come to know the principles within this book as the actual truth - "in the beginning was The Word," says the Bible - said another way, Consciousness, having conjured the idea of a world of form, brought it into being with the idea itself. The same Consciousness, when extended into forms, has this same capability, filtered through the physics of the dream world we are experiencing. We cannot create instantly, because minds are subscribed to and forms are subsequently subject to the element of time which is just a concept of this dream. So, to clean up one's word, including the words of thoughts, and subsequently learn the lessons remaining for the soul (that little drop of Consciousness which is still within the larger ocean of Consciousness), may take some time, but does not necessarily require it. It is up to us and ultimately Divine Will, and it will depend upon our willingness to surrender in the continually unfolding present moment.

## "Bad" Things in the World of Form

Recalling once again the concepts of the Bible, when God created the world, it was said that "He" saw that it was good. Put another and less conceptual way, when Consciousness conceived of the world, it did it intentionally - the chaos and the outcomes humans deem as negative are a part of the complete experience of life on earth. All other beings on earth go with the flow - it is humans who have constructed the idea that "bad" weather is bad and should make us feel gloom, that the passing away of another human form should be cause for years or lifetimes of grief, that any one thing is better than another thing. When we are able to drop such erroneous ideas and live in our true nature, we see that while we might grieve for a time as the human part we play, as Consciousness we contain all human lives, past and present, simultaneously. Nothing dies, nothing is born - all is recycled as parts of this experience, and the very same life force is a constant. Thank goodness our happiness need not be wrapped up in earthly things, every single one of them cracked and bruised and ready to decay. What a blessing to see the decaying world in contrast to our timeless perfection. We are at our essence whole and complete - we are not simply here as one individual with one shot at a full life, and using it to pick fights and create division. This is merely one experience had by one bit of Consciousness which is not separate from the whole. Beneath this experiment is that which needs no tweaking, and forms capable of love must come from love. "Hate," as we've come to call it, is merely a perceived disconnection from that love, just as darkness is nothing but a lack of light. There is Consciousness, and the experience of an apparent lack of Consciousness.

### What a Joke

When we realize that despite appearances, we do not have skin in this game, it becomes rather funny that our true identity is timeless, deathless love itself and yet these human avatars so rarely hit the mark and achieve true selfless love (even then, it's not the human achieving it). This is only funny if at the core of all this, nobody is being harmed - if all this suffering is ultimately real, it's not a joke. When we realize all is well and drop the "other," drop the words and concepts for "evil," "shame," "guilt," and "blame," we understand the ultimate mission - all human forms are cooperating in the obscuring of and ultimate returning to the source of all love and happiness that has been with us, as us, this entire time. Despite how it looks, our true and essential self is actually having quite a lovely time on this journey, because it knows no "other."

It can seem callous to laugh at the world when "others" are seemingly suffering so much. We can acknowledge the suffering of the world of form, the thing that so many human characters are playing out, and many are subjecting plant and animal characters to as well. On the surface, it looks very sad. But this is not where we are looking, and why just a slight recalibration in our vision is essential to realization of the true nature of reality. When the truth is seen, we see it deeply, beyond form. It is not something which can be seen by the eyes or heard by the ears. This is why it is said that this is the only truth which can be verified - it is the only one that does not rely on our equipment but is experienced directly when there is an absence of bias in the space of our attention.

I used to experience frustration when I would witness spiritual teachers seemingly oblivious to the world around them, seemingly enjoying endless financial resources and ample time on their hands with which to enjoy life, unlike "the rest of us." Mind was of course "othering" them without knowing anything of the experience which led them to where they are today. The darkness within my character, the part that thought enlightenment was impossible, wanted to bring others down to my level - *they must be lying, they can only be happy because they're ignoring others' pain*. When we find reality truly funny, we are not laughing at others from a place of being incapable of experiencing deep pain and empathy. We are laughing because we have been exactly there, and because that other is all of us and none of us, and we see that all suffering is illusory. You have believed you are a body simply because it is what you have been told and it's how things appear - it's exactly the way the world was designed, to "trick" its own creator, the real you, into experiencing its boundaries as real. Now it's so hard to see what would have been apparent if socialization had not boxed in the experience, because all of the thoughts have been conceived of based on that core belief. The individual human mind emerged from stimuli, from input, from a desire to survive within a community. If there were no words to form concepts, there could be no thoughts, and if there were no thoughts, there would be no basis for problems - an idea invented by humans. Words came to identify things, then each other, then more complicated concepts, more and more intricate feelings, and so on. Before that, there were no negative feelings beyond the primal and fleeting, and then enters the argument of whether those could be called negative at all. One could see their face in a pool of water without judgment or preoccupation. All of this is as an experiment with a new way to process experience, and humans are not at all well-adjusted to this level of internal activity. That's it, and this in itself makes all humans beyond judgment. This world is not presently set up for sanity - but we, as our essential self, never lose it for a second. When we act as our true self, when the "others" vanish, there is not one thing to "lose one's mind" about, and yet in another way it is lost, leaving behind all it covered up.

### The Circus and the One-Handed Clap

We are living through a time said to have unprecedented political strife and perceived danger, brought on by more invasive and frequent methods of exposure to divisive conversation in our very homes and even in the bathtub. The way we are taking in information is diminishing our ability to consent to what we experience, from the perspective of the character being played - one minute we are weeping at a sentimental ad, the next we are incensed upon seeing a news clip, the next we read a suggestion for a calming exercise and perhaps this even annoys us. We are capable of creating for ourselves, but we are more plugged into someone else's creations than ever before. We experience that critical thinking and peace of mind are suffering as a result, with many to most feeling our very sense of who we are is more lost than ever. And of course, when we feel this way, the aspect of the mind that wants to feel separate will look for more "others" upon whom to blame this scenario - "the Right/Left is killing our country, people who leave the water on while brushing their teeth are destroying the environment, if you don't use your remaining threads of sanity and energy to actively fight against [insert contentious subject] I can't be associated with you." Arguments are being had with strangers on the internet for no apparent reason but to vent our anger, and in fact, as we are witnessing, this venting isn't helping us to feel better in the least. It is exactly like a workout for our anger - the anger muscle becomes tired for a bit, but comes back stronger, more reinforced. Egos are being reinforced and they thrive on it.

As further strife appears to be promising itself in our uncertain future, it is time to experience the "one-handed clap." This Buddhist concept points to the fact that without two hands, without the "other," there can be no resistance to meet with - when we see all as one, all we experience is the one true Self, and so there is nothing to create friction or noise with.

Notice that in an argument, it takes two to have any ongoing resistance. Notice that even within one's own mind, an "other" has been created in order to create internal tension, and without that other, there can be no opposition - there would be peace. Now, notice that without that opposition, that in refusing to feed these internal energies, both sides will subside or retreat. Take this concept and apply it to the vast chaos of social media. If 10% of the participants in these unprecedented arguments ceased their efforts, we could not limit the outcome to the claim that 10% of arguments would cease, mathematically or otherwise. In fact, the world would change so drastically that we might say the problem of social media strife no longer exists. The same is true of society at large - if only 1% of society consisted of "enlightened" characters, the ripples sent out from all resultant actions would be immeasurable. Because I have chosen to attract these kinds of conversations in the way I speak and the places I meet people, I am living a life where most of the people I speak to wish to be within what would currently be an outlying group of humans who choose to live against the grain - they simply don't yet know how, from lack of accessible models or access to inner wisdom. This is why when we attempt to change the world, we are heading in the wrong direction - if you drop out of the struggle and play the part of one who helps one hundred through effortless modeling, you have done far more than you ever would have burning yourself at both ends to fit into the societal norm of struggle, or forcing egoic "help" onto unwilling others.

I experienced this change firsthand when I removed myself from social media for three months. There was not simply a reduction in negative stimuli - I had to do something else with the time that had previously been spent that way. On my hikes, in meeting up with new friends, in my extra hours of yoga, again I found that the life gained could not simply be quantified in hours. I was meeting people who were not on social media, I was falling out of touch with those who did not engage with me outside of the platform, I was losing the sense that what happened needed a witness other than myself in order to be valid or meaningful, and the sense of isolation at seeing everyone's lives lived without me was completely dropped. I still knew that lives were being lived without me, but my attention was not being placed there, and so it reached the point of having no effect on me. What's more, I had gained immense energy to apply to my favorite projects, and my sense of purpose in life began to clarify without all the noise. After those few months, when I briefly logged on to use one of the platform's secondary functions, my threshold for drama had lowered significantly, and my brief and habitual surfing resulted in my quickly removing the whole thing from my devices once again. What had seemed necessary was now so obviously pointless in the light of newly developed discernment, which developed naturally when the mind was not being bombarded with the views of others.

Contrary to the mind's typical conclusion, a lack of resistance to what others are doing does not equate to inaction. Spiritual leaders are sometimes criticized for their lack of involvement in social justice or other efforts, and indeed this mind harbored an inner resistance when I saw apparent inaction from my favorite teachers. This is more of the mind's binary workings, determining that one is either "with us" or "with them," either involved or apathetic. My time heavily involved in activism without a high level of discernment led my mind to be incredibly divisive, and living with such a mind led me to be too tired to do the work of my heart, constantly struggling with burnout. Beyond this, I witnessed two people within the local activism community alone die within one year, one intentionally and another somewhat intentionally through severely destructive lifestyle choices. The constant fighting, struggling, and othering that was occurring within this particular circle, not to mention the sense that one never knew where the lines of propriety and acceptability had been drawn, led to the decision to shift my efforts to what truly helped me to be better. In choosing love and releasing limiting beliefs, in no longer reacting to what I see, I send out ripples which will continue to spread after this body is done. When I live with ease, I am able to apply my energy to my preferred method of action - speaking about the "spiritual" solution to the world's practical and ultimately illusory problems. I no longer assume that I as Heather know so much that I can tell others how to get involved or when to stay away - I know that there is only one surprisingly inclusive truth, and the rest has been constructed by humans as part of the cause and effect machine called the mind. When one truly looks at human life from the beginning and sees the way it has shifted, it becomes less and less possible to believe one knows anything except that which is directly experienced without bias or limited perception. To live life without judgment, without vilifying the "other," is to live as the free, loving Awareness that you are.

### Looking For A Fight

I'm issuing a personal challenge to you (fighting words already) - notice the part of you that likes to argue. Notice the inner conflict that exists, the pointlessness of that, and yet the prevalence, often just under or barely within the radar of your attention. Somehow it has escaped our notice that if at least two voices exist within us, we cannot be both of them. In truth, we are neither of them, and neither of them are really there - we are watching it all go down, observing these fights. So what is it that is starting the fights? It is the mind, the ego. And what is the ego? There is no physical location for this entity - it exists solely in the thoughts that flood your attention. So what happens when those thoughts cease or are ignored? Where does that entity go?

The mind subsists solely on the energy fed to it - you are powering your reality with your attention. To ensure that there is a consistent supply, the mind produces thoughts of a false binary - good and bad, you and them - and all the shame and blame that go with it. In reality, there are no lazy people, no selfish people, no angry people. None are argumentative, none are not living up to potential. We've made all of this up based on what our parents made up, based on what their parents made up. Recognizing that humans are just ideas that Awareness had, that they are acting out a play until we realize the play exists, is to realize that we do not truly take on any of the identifying traits of the play. If you come into a new human character as a baby in a family of abuse, the character will take on the traits of the environment until it is decided not to. Some humans decide quickly they want to be everything their family is not, and may become that unintentionally anyway. The body begins with certain capabilities and circumstances, but we don't own that body - we are borrowing it, using it - and all the traits pertaining to it do not define us. So, when we believe ourselves superior because we broke from our traits earlier than someone else, we are showing our ignorance of that struggle and inherent capabilities - we limit ourselves with the very thought of it. Those with "anger issues" experienced anger along with events which caused them to squash their feelings. That anger, trapped in the body, carries its own energy signature, being presented again by the body which seeks to release it, so the anger comes up periodically or even daily, or perhaps it is even constantly present, and each time we have the choice - feed Awareness, or feed the anger. Those seemingly without anger will be coming from a number of backgrounds, possibly including a bodymind that is not disposed to generate great anger, an environment which made it safe or sufficiently motivating to move past that anger, or perhaps they simply did not need to suppress anger as children, so they are not visited by those unresolved processes in the body. Looking at someone who struggles with anger and deeming yourself better at handling yours is to create an "other" and bolster a self which is made entirely of illusion. After all, the Consciousness playing that character is also playing "your" character - they're both you.

### There Is No Enemy

The time in which we are living seems to offer us more opportunities than ever to change our life circumstances - one well-timed video and we can quit our job; one public spectacle and we have the opportunity to run for public office. The media cycle and unlimited access to it make all of this possible. However, this has brought to many a nearly 24-hour cycle of churning, as the mind tries to compete and vie for attention as though life depends on it. This simultaneously brings about an ambivalence in the young, inheriting a seemingly doomed earth with unattainable standards, wishing to scrap the whole thing and retreat to the mountains alone yet incapable of freeing themselves from a digital world saturated with others' opinions. Somehow the system designed to address the trading of basic goods has made it more difficult than ever for a human being to thrive.

If only we could realize that we, in one life or another, have contributed to the present state of things - that there exists no enemy, and no need to protect oneself over another. If only we realized that, at the deepest level, there is absolutely no separation of any kind between forms - that we are just filtered sections of the same thing having different experiences. If only, all at once, we could take a collective deep breath and sigh out our beliefs, going forward from that moment without any concern for what "others" do and how we stack up to it. If we could achieve that, we could see others' actions as inspiration, never provoking jealousy, conformity, or isolation.

We may view those who have hurt others to get ahead in life as our enemies, as those to avoid, to fear, to judge. While we certainly have the option of staying away, especially when we are in the infancy of our journey and the mind is painting a picture of great suffering, all resistance just perpetuates these stories. What's more, we miss the point - that to live with a mind that is so fearful that the best it can do is to take, to continually hurt oneself by hurting "others" who are extensions of you, is its own punishment, and more than sufficient. Anything above this only perpetuates the state of aloneness and isolation that has led someone to this level of survival mode, to continue gaining, acquiring, and adding to one's sense of self, unable to stop. To paraphrase Viktor Frankl, the Holocaust survivor, psychiatrist, and existential author, "in a state of true inspiration and creativity, success is not pursued - rather, it ensues." It must be understood that in this scenario, one pursues their work from a place of effortless enjoyment - in this state of effortlessness, one's work is infused with inspiration and intuition, never clouded by the thinking mind's desire to avoid negative outcomes in their many forms. Any activity more difficult than effortless perpetuates struggle and depletion, and this can be understood by all who are willing. When you experience this, no matter how uneven the tables seem, to plot revenge or to get ahead is to cause harm to yourself, and to release these notions is to ensure your own happiness - to settle the score, to "win."

I spent years perceiving slights and rejection everywhere. I had been rejected or abandoned by so many, according to the mind, and I was all alone in the Universe. As a result, I became preemptively critical of others, ready to drop friendships at the first sign of being taken for granted, and subsequently pitying myself when friendships fell apart over very little. I had not given of my true self, of pure love, and others saw that. My friendships were limited by the mind, out of fear of being hurt. I hurt myself in an effort to bolster and protect. In this way, I also played into the false narratives placed upon me - I certainly appeared difficult and contentious to those unwilling to look deeper, and this only frustrated me further.

When I finally stepped back, I noticed that nothing was personal. I realized that my supposed offenders were suffering for the same reasons I was - it followed that they were likely taking my personal pleas for love as attacks too, all through their own limited lenses and fear of rejection. We were all rejecting each other in alternation. When I realized this, I saw that my own view was the very thing making me unhappy. I could not change the way others contributed to relationship dynamics, but I could mend what I could through non-reactive and loving consciousness, and make space between those unwilling to cease hurtful behavior and choose love amidst the fear. What's more, I saw my true identity - having absolutely nothing to do with any of the claims laid against me over the years. When it was no longer personal, it just didn't matter. My true identity was wholeness, happiness, and joy. I would accept nothing less into my beliefs. When I dropped the beliefs which no longer served me, I no longer saw slights and rejection where I had before. My very energy changed, and the humans who sought to build up and love their friends became attracted to that within me that they recognized in themselves. It was really that easy. This world is entirely of your creation, and you can create a world without enemies and others, simple as that.

# CHAPTER FOUR

## TAKING RESPONSIBILITY

**Louise Hay**

Years ago, I embraced the teacher Louise Hay at a time when I needed her teachings most. Her motherly delivery soothed me, and when she would say that she wished the word "should" was dropped completely from our vocabulary, I let out a little cheer inside. While she seems to have been of a nondual understanding, in her talks she would allude to but not explicitly speak on certain aspects of the journey, her message having been tailored to the average reader of the mid-1980s.

While in theory I understand that in each human experience, with limitless time and energy to apply toward the endeavor, one can attain what is called enlightenment by simply going inward, I know that most people have jobs, families, and other responsibilities which, on the surface level, require time, attention, and energy such that there seems not to be any remaining for the full-bodied practice of inquiry into the self. I know it can be difficult at first to muster the freedom of mind to release attachment to these constructs, so it is hard to see outside the status quo. What we need, and what is subsequently being given to us, are lessons with clear, concise pointing to the Truth that minimizes the number of detours we end up taking, without eliminating any of the essential parts of the journey.

In her work, Hay stresses the importance of taking responsibility for our life circumstances. This is quite distinct from taking the blame for them or taking on shame for how things have turned out so far. It is quite the opposite - when we realize that all of our suffering has been, in one way or another, of our own creation, we see that it can all change with one decision to correct our course.

I had not known how to grieve as a young adult when my mother died. I had not known how to juggle this grief with my studies as a freshman in college, where nobody knew or cared. I ran away to Hawai'i, to the one person who took the time to ask how I was doing, and we got married there. When he showed himself as having been compromised by his own experiences and unable to be the rock I had expected, the entire bottom of my life fell out. He was discharged from the military, we were sent home to Ohio, and upon arriving, I entered into a new job right away, found a job for him, and pushed past that phase believing time alone would heal. The job became untenable, I went back to school while maintaining my job, I was laid off just after finishing school, and I started my work as a massage therapist where I experienced burnout and a perceived lack of success for years. When ten years of marriage resulted in an amicable split, it upset many people in my inner circle and I found myself navigating it alone. I dated for years and nothing stuck. I started a business and a global virus wiped it out just when things were feeling properly established. Reconnecting with my best friend from college, it seemed I would gain a family, stability, and love - I gained none of this but endured the most unhealthy relationship of my life, which didn't stop me from allowing the relationship to continue to deepen until I found myself feeling trapped in the commitments I'd made.

Until awakening began to unfold, this had been the sob story that the attention had been fixed upon. How could so many things go wrong for one person? How, when I was responsible, generous to those I was comfortable with, and deserving of trust, was I living this life? Suddenly, reciting this story to myself one day, I heard "the tone," felt "the feeling" - the tension and lack present when the inner actor in the mind is on full display, weaving a tale of woe. I felt the constriction in the chest, I noticed that part of me that was attached to, even enjoying the misery, and all was clear. I had not introduced self-pitying beliefs to myself, but I had adopted them. I did not abandon myself, but I did retreat from the help available to me, having taken on the idea that it was weak to express one's grief and needs, or feeling unsafe entering into an agreement where I would owe someone an unknown debt to be repaid at their leisure. I didn't get myself or anyone else discharged, but I chose a partner with a lack of career ambition and expected different. I remained in the connection for nearly ten years after the initial incident, reinforcing the idea that I would stay through anything and allowing it to continue to shape my life. I actively chose to seek another partner, rather than to redirect more of my time into personal growth, friendship-building, and things I generally enjoyed doing. I dated from a place of incompleteness, which I had not invented but had bought into. When my business was shuttered for Covid, my mind drove itself crazy with resentment at a perceived lack of support, all while being fully capable of being the love and support I needed. And each moment that I stayed in an unhealthy relationship was a moment that I was being dishonest with myself and forcing a circumstance, the next in a long line of fear-based decisions.

Finally, in this moment, the cycle could no longer perpetuate itself - I no longer believed the mind's tales of woe. All opportunity for happiness had been just behind my pain the entire time despite my hearing hundreds of times that "joy is just behind the pain" in some form or another. Suddenly, asking myself the question *what would I have done had I not acted out of fear* presented a laundry list of possibilities - joined a hiking group, learned about primitive camping, looked at my fears, painted, more yoga - this was a life I liked the sound of. The only reason this had not materialized was my buy-in to thoughts that were never true - that I was lonely, incomplete, that friends couldn't be counted upon for active relationships like romantic partners could. Never could I go back to the habitual ways of the identity I had constructed. I could refine the Heather Experience by knowingly being what I truly was - when I believed myself to be whole, complete, and Divine, the idea of loneliness was seen for exactly what it was - a human construct based on a misunderstanding.

It has become truly amusing noticing the turnings of the mind from a detached vantage point. When old patterns begin to act themselves out, like when someone doesn't seem to see how astounding this constructed personality is, I'll hear "who cares, I have other friends," "I am intelligent! I am worth getting to know! They will regret it!" before the attention shifts back to Awareness and I remember that it actually doesn't matter how intelligent this character has turned out to be, how many friends there are, or whether others' insults about this constructed self are accurate or false in a relative sense. It all pertains to the surface level and reflects how much buy-in there is into a constructed reality, even after significant re-training efforts.

Louise Hay experienced abuse, poverty, and severe health issues in her young life. She described herself as becoming a complaining and negative person before she developed cancer, despite her best efforts to heal and become a coach herself, and decided it was time to take her healing journey much more seriously. She simultaneously fed her body only good foods and began forgiving every transgression she'd hung onto in her mind, stopping herself from speaking and eventually even thinking negatively, not through suppression but by talking back to her words and thoughts. She healed her cancer without medical treatment within months, and her relatively new coaching practice was taken to new heights. She eventually wrote the bestseller "You Can Heal Your Life" and enjoyed a meaningful practice and good health for decades more.

Louise Hay is widely criticized for her "overly simplistic" approach to healing, and speaks to this in her subsequent books. Without completely opening to the concepts and practices, people would chant her famous affirmations several times and report nothing having happened. Conversely, there were numerous accounts within her in-person talks of spontaneous healing having occurred within certain bodies, including one account she mentions of a woman's body curing itself of breast cancer in the same moment that she experienced deep resonance with a statement that was just what she needed to hear. In the context of the great many "medical miracles" reported in association with the mind suddenly getting fully on board with a forward-looking approach to healing, this is no surprise, and yet the seemingly magical nature of it still causes us to think "it can't be that simple, one must still depend on some slim chance of being 'chosen' in one way or other for this to happen." As someone who has repeatedly felt the healing within my own body from lesser concerns like acid reflux, food sensitivities, joint issues, and unexplained weight gain, I can tell you there is no proving this. One must prove this to themselves, and it may require first practicing in small ways and moving up to the things that appear as miracles to us. Humanity is on the brink of having suffered enough and created a dysfunctional enough societal structure to be willing to consider deeply that what they think is true may not be true - to take responsibility for one's own unconsciousness of experience, and to see that the collective state of consciousness reflects the individual state, is how we find our way home.

## John F. Barnes

John Barnes was an athlete and physical therapist when he experienced a fracture in one of his vertebrae, leaving him with sometimes unbearable pain and severely limited functionality. John saw many specialists for his concerns, and would not accept the "incurable" prognosis given to him repeatedly. He decided to heal himself and studied Traditional Chinese Medicine, massage therapy, energy work, and quantum physics among other modalities, until he began to understand what was truly at play behind his pain - his bodymind's own resistance. He developed a method called Myofascial Release Therapy, which is now practiced by medical professionals worldwide, through the painstaking and years-long trial and error with his own body, until he came to understand that the body could heal itself rapidly through a state of presence coupled with physical traction which could be facilitated by a highly competent and intuitive practitioner but must ultimately be brought about by a willingness and openness on the part of both the therapist and the patient. When the patient was truly willing to heal, it could result in what would be called miraculous results. Some of these results include the healing of colitis, cancer, anxiety, depression, scar tissue, heart conditions, and many to most other maladies.

What could have simply devolved into a sedentary life full of bitterness became a successful healing practice, a profoundly impactful training program, and complete or nearly complete healing to his injuries, allowing John to engage in a physically demanding profession well into advanced age. He could certainly be viewed as disadvantaged in the journey of self-healing, and while not all dis-eases can be or are meant to be healed in this lifetime, a great deal we have deemed unhealable are still left to our personal responsibility - will we buy the story or will we plug the power of the mind, via our attention, into a socket of our own creation?

Note: There is no judgment implied in these illustrations. The complex cause and effect machine we call karma leads to different people feeling different ways about different things so constantly that none of us can keep up with the contradiction in it all, and while one cannot begin to fathom all the contributors to the emotional states that might keep one from pursuing their own healing, we know that this state exists for a reason. There is no way one can judge another based on karmic origins and outcomes. All of this is simply to say: in each and every moment, you have a choice to diverge from your whitewater rafting trip in the stream of karma where you've been paddling endlessly toward survival, instead of watching the current ebb, flow, and pass by from the shore. This choice becomes even more pronounced once you have been made aware of it, but even before then, in every moment, the real you has been there capable of being seen if only space was given. If your true nature is not realized within this lifetime, that is not your fault - it is, however, your responsibility, and within your power in this moment, to decide if you will diverge from the stream of karma to see what is closer even than right in front of you.

**You**

Do you suffer from acid reflux but refuse to cut out tomatoes, tight pants, and sugar? Have you decided anxiety is a disorder that has simply "happened to you" from out of nowhere with no clear cause, and decided to medicate and attach it to the story of "you?" Do you want to be a computer programmer but refuse to take a coding class because it will cut into your "checkout time" after work? This is simple conditioning. When we realize that minds were designed to specialize the more we train on the same old thoughts, the mind says, "I don't want to play a game I can't win." This is just another thought, one that it has been trained by society to think. Step back from that thought, notice the perpetual nature of it and others, let go of the momentum of this way, and you will begin to see that you do have a choice - you can just change course. You are also not to blame - you are playing a game where you were seemingly born into all the makings of the character, just like everyone else. When we know this, we stop blaming ourselves, and it becomes much easier to accept accountability - we don't need to punish ourselves or feel bad.

Ultimately, taking responsibility is something that occurs at the human level. It is a refinement of thought, a releasing of stories and resistance. In the end, there is no person who has to take responsibility, but a character powered by Consciousness. So, we do this work with a grain of salt - we are using the mind to deconstruct itself.

# CHAPTER FIVE

## THE DEEP DIVE INTO LOVE

There are countless reasons attributed to the apparent lack of love in today's society. Some say that ever since the Industrial Revolution and the advent of rubberized shoe soles as well as the expansion of cities with concrete and pavement as far as the eye can see, we have been largely separated from contact with the earth, and with the healing frequency of that earth. Those who believe this find that when they make contact with the earth daily, even if it is through bedsheets which plug into an electrical outlet or special shoes that keep us in contact with those lovely 7.83 Hertz, that their health and sanity is restored. Some suggest this lack of love is due to a lack of the touch we naturally need as humans, while others insist that a society where we do not touch one another in any way without consent is the healthiest and most loving. Others attribute this lack of love to the popularization of television shows with false ideas about life; still others attribute it to violent video games, or excess screen time by children in past decades. All of these have relative merit when we look through the lens of the world of form, taking physics into account - they are cooperating toward the ends we are looking to avoid, but they are not the direct causes.

There is only one root cause for a lack of love in society - the apparent lack of love within oneself, the disconnect from our loving nature through the belief that we are the self that we have constructed from a place of fear and need. All other causes, while relatively and conditionally true at best, manifest themselves from this one. As such, each of them is subject to the ability to realize the Divinity within, which IS the one self. When the human form is introduced to the game of life on earth, it goes live with the power to co-create the Universe. The power isn't the human's - it's yours, Consciousness. When the mind runs amok, all sorts of things that we don't intend to create are created. We unintentionally cause misery within our own family units because we don't realize how unhappy we are or consider it a given; we contribute to a cold and unfeeling world when we walk around stuck in our own thoughts; and we unintentionally create circumstances which lead to chaos all around us by believing that the world is chaotic, anger-inducing, scary, or wrong.

Love, as it truly is, does not require reciprocation of any kind, because it is a reward to the giver, and effortless to give. When you feel that all you do is pour out love and get none back, what you are giving is not love - it is conditional affection or service. When you feel empty of love, you are subscribing to the idea that your own love does not or cannot feed and fill you, and you are allowing yourself to be emptied in hopes someone else will fill your cup. In truth, only the body heals itself, only the love of Awareness can heal the mind, and only you can work out your own liberation from suffering. Only your own love, the love of the Divine which many feel has been ripped from them or is somehow elusive, can fill the humanly spaces left by mistaken identity. It doesn't matter if this is under the label of Christianity or Buddhism, the mechanism of giving all to God or Consciousness has the same impact on the bodymind if we do it from pure love and understand that we are all one. There is nobody coming to save you from your suffering in this lifetime, and this is the best news one can hear, when heard cleanly. Pure Awareness, your true identity, requires no savior, requires no input, because it is all-knowing and pure love itself. That we are our own savior right here and now is the most beautiful and empowering truth, and one which I have seen manifest itself as peaceful bliss over and over as realization of an already existing and constant awakened state has deepened within. This is not something you will need to cultivate over time by adding things to yourself - simply remove the extraneous and false idea that your identity is comprised of a small individual person living on earth, allow Awareness to show itself, and love will flood the space you've made. The more space you make, the more the values and thoughts acquired here are released, the more silence exists to hear the call of love. While my way of describing this might sound somewhat poetic, as do the messages echoing the same sentiment throughout time, this is not a poetic or esoteric idea. It is the most real, most true and most attainable thing in life, though the mind certainly tells another story - your true nature is love itself. If you can avoid making the detour of allowing the ego to turn this into a long and drawn out process, of believing these lessons to be overly simplistic or far-fetched or not for you, you will save yourself years of exercises refining and purifying the mind in preparation. This is why self-realization through nonduality is often called the Direct Path, and why in these pages we work with both a minimized indirect approach as well as the direct approach. We only "need" the indirect approach as long as there is the belief it is needed.

### Love is the Healer

During my studies as a Myofascial Release Therapist under John Barnes, I learned a great deal about the body's connective tissue and how it really functions and heals. This work incorporates several aspects of the physics of the world of form, including quantum physics' discovery of the true state of matter as well as the Piezoelectric Phenomenon. Scientists have caught up with the wisdom of indigenous peoples and Gautama Buddha, who discovered through direct observation completely devoid of bias that the human body was not solid, but made up of energy which is reformed each and every second and can be manipulated by the mind. Many times during extended meditation sessions and sometimes spontaneously, the solidity of the human body will begin to fall away as attention is successfully diverted from what mind says it knows about life. Just like an ill-fitting virtual reality headset suddenly allowing rays of light to shine in, suddenly bits of evidence of a world beyond what is projecting onto the screen of life become visible, palpable. In the Piezoelectric Phenomenon, which says that placing and holding pressure on a viscous object creates an electric charge, and that over time this pressure will change the structure of the object, we can begin to understand how the supposedly magical "laying on of hands" tradition is representative of the power of loving and present human touch paired with openness to the possibility to initiate healing in the body. In a sense, this work harnesses the power of Reiki or other energy healing work while also employing a known physical phenomenon to spur things on. In this way, the body can be jumpstarted into the process of rearranging itself, and depending upon the state of the mind, which yoga describes as a distinct layer of the body occupying the same space but functioning from another dimension, that rearranged state could be that of a completely healed body. John discovered that when one waited and felt the body, rather than trying to force through the tissue like the "pain is gain" techniques so many request, believing results can only be had through dramatic settings, one was able to interact with the tissue without engaging the body's tendency to recoil and protect. In being gentle, slow, and informed in one's precise application of pressure in a specific direction and area based on the signs the body provided, one could return life-giving fluid to a frozen shoulder, could return blood flow to a scarred area, could even heal cancer in a supposedly terminal patient.

In his book "How Healing Works," Dr. Wayne Jonas, director of the Office of Alternative Medicine at the National Institutes of Health from 1995 to 1999, spoke of his experience with Western medicine being challenged when he visited Traditional Chinese Medicine hospitals and Ayurvedic clinics in the East, begrudgingly acknowledging that the treatment methods offered by these branches of medicine often seemed as effective or better than Western methods. What he discovered over the cross-examination of many double blind studies was that incorporating the Placebo Effect, which has been shown over time to be responsible for a whopping 80% of healing in medicine overall, offering patients ample outdoor time, a peaceful setting, and plenty of time to interact with supportive family, these settings for healing facilitated much better results than the sterile, chaotic, and isolated Western hospitals. When the patient felt loved and cared for, when they felt trust in their caregivers, and when they understood and resonated with their treatment, their healing was much improved over their Western counterparts. Now just imagine how this is enhanced when we apply an unconditional sense of wellbeing at understanding that, while supportive family is great, I am my own love and healing, whether shining through an "other" or not.

When Louise Hay traveled giving talks about how to heal one's own health using the mind, she would implore her students with urgency to begin to forgive their supposed trespassers as soon as they could, before they were mired by dis-ease and subsequent panic in the body. In embodying love, all fear must dissolve, and with it the dis-ease that was being perpetuated by constant tension and blockages. For all our technology, for all the complicated modalities of healing, it is being shown to be that simple.

## Forgiveness as a Foundation

I struggled for a long time with forgiveness - I thought it was something that my transgressors didn't deserve without a genuine apology and changed behavior, letting them off too easily. It wasn't until I was grieving the loss of several relationships years ago when I developed all sorts of symptoms I thought I had licked almost two decades ago, from acid reflux to migraines to digestive issues to heart palpitations to chest and upper abdomen tightness to fatigue, that I finally decided to relent and consider the process deeply. From my experience with yoga and bodywork, I knew that suppressed emotion was bringing these symptoms about (this is not the same as saying it was all in my head, a dismissive and blame-filled expression) - what I didn't realize was that I had suppressed a great deal of my anger for years, too afraid to express myself, and built up more and more resentment at feeling so stifled. When I realized this, I knew that I needed to forgive my transgressors, and in considering my own role in the unhealthy relationships, and the effort it was taking to build up a story around my villains to preserve a sense of victimhood and of being right, I knew it was time to level up.

When I tried to forgive the apparently remorseless, it felt impossible. I would sit and say to myself - "I forgive them and I release my anger." Nothing happened. I began to despair at the process which I had found relief in for years, when I finally realized that I had been hiding details of events from myself. In addition to the genuinely unhealthy aspects of relationships, mind been causing a great deal of this fear through endless commentary, in order to ensure I would make the right decisions and leave unhealthy situations. I didn't trust myself to make the right decision if my suffering was below a certain threshold, so I kept it above that level consistently. Despite my work in establishing healthy boundaries in recent years, the mind was pulling an old trick - it dredged up thoughts relating to a lack of trust in myself from years past when boundaries had been nonexistent to me. What's more, I had ignored some very telling signs in recent relationships, so it really looked as though I couldn't be trusted. Add to this the lies I had internalized over a lifetime, and who could blame me for a lack of clarity? In reality, I had simply been moving from one fire to another, trying to escape one bad situation by quickly jumping into the next. When I saw this, compassion flooded in - the mind had done all this in its wish to keep the entity called "me" safe. It was mistaken, sorely so, but it had always wished to keep itself, the small me, safe.

With this realization under my belt and a little time to allow my nervous system to attune to an environment of peace and patience, I was able to forgive myself for what I hadn't known. I had certainly learned from my suffering, and it was very clear even to the critical aspect of my mind that I did everything from a wish to live a happy and peaceful life. The fact that the outcome had not matched the intention did not mean that I should be subject to additional punishment via negative thinking - I could move on!

Having forgiven myself, life opened up. Guilt and guarding subsided, and I began to enjoy life again. One morning just after waking, I suddenly felt ready to forgive those I felt had severely hurt me, to release the energy that was hurting my body. Suddenly, it was as if none of it had happened - mind no longer ruminated on it and it was as though I had never been injured. In fact, I had not - the deeper part of me that was beginning to make itself known as I softened was not subject to harm by anyone or anything. It was shortly after this time that deeper realization of the self started unfolding more quickly, and with that, the pain associated with these events quickly began to fade from memory. At times the feelings and patterns would resurface, and at times the mind would present old roadblocks again, but each time met with greater Awareness, and each time a little weaker. With this, the pain in the chest, digestive concerns, palpitations, and fatigue quickly began to fade, and the body was on its way to healing itself, a simple shift in attention having cleared the way.

Forgiveness, like personal responsibility, is taking place at the personal level. It is an intermediary step, one of clearing up our understanding. Ultimately, there is nothing and nobody to forgive. We will work with this later.

### Include Yourself in the Equation

If you feel that you are loving and not getting it back in return, you are taking part in a common practice called affection; this is different from love. You are pouring out with the expectation of return based on how you think a relationship should go; true love does not deplete you when it is given because it does not require any acts to take place, though they may certainly ensue. I like to imagine a cup already full and overflowing when I think of how to love - a naturally occurring inner force, it can recognize when love is not being returned and yet it feels no sadness nor reflection upon itself - it sees the stifled love and the frustrated desire to be happy beneath the misguided words and actions; it feels no insecurity. This is the source of excellent boundaries and the ability to be fierce yet gentle when needed.

It is okay to allow the bottom to fall out for others, even when you have a strong urge to help. When you see that someone is struggling and does not yet have the instinct to save themselves, they are living out their karma - a combination of inherited and chosen circumstances for the soul's education. The Divine within them is living this life on purpose, to understand this precise angle of suffering and to return to ultimate love even through these circumstances. Suffering is the red flag that tells us we are off the path, and the soul will not experience this level of suffering via the human, this crisis point which tells us enough is enough, when it is continually bailed out or otherwise allowed to continue its behavior - rather, it recognizes that it can play the game of being bailed out, of testing limits, perpetuating further experiments in this way. When we allow someone to fail or to see our impenetrable limits, when we release attachment to their life circumstances going a certain way and recognize that it is theirs to live as they wish unless they choose to abuse their surface level free will to hurt others, we give them the opportunity to experience the autonomy of the Creator, and it has the opportunity of emerging in a profound way. I am grateful for the times when I was told "no" - these instances directly resulted in the recognition of my own strength, and ultimately my true identity. Saying no from a place of caring is love; expending energy to appear nice or generous or to not be left alone is not love but fear, and perpetuates more of the same. Recognize this and return to yourself - the Infinite Divine Consciousness giving life to all things.

**Love From a Distance**

Part of loving is knowing when to be that from a distance. As I researched love years ago, hearing about its power to transform formerly dysfunctional relationships, I caused myself great pain trying to change those around me or to "love them into consciousness" when I wasn't there myself. Even if one is fully awakened, at times the presence of that awakened state near a highly unconscious person can elicit a resistant response - can drive the unconscious people around us bonkers - or more likely, along our journey their antics can make us feel like we're going bonkers. In "The Artist's Way," a timeless work on bringing out the inner Creator, Julia Cameron writes of the artist who is afraid to fully embody their journey seeking out the "crazy-makers" - those we know on some level will delay, distract, and drive us crazy. We do all of this in an unconscious effort to deflect from our fear of our own power - the mind cannot conceive of it, and the more we identify as the mind, the less it makes sense. On your way to awakening, these kinds of codependent relationships may dissolve, or you may find that it is best to create distance between you and another on the form level. This is a wonderful way to love yourself; though you have experienced being born into a family and a community, and if you can it is good to preserve those ties, your one go-round in this body can be spent being loved and appreciated, and as you are the Infinite, there is no reason for you to compromise on this. If you are in contact with those who would see only your worst, who are committed to misunderstanding or subtly sabotaging you, you are under no spiritual or form-based obligation or contract to "try to make them see" the beauty of you, and attempting to do so is just ego wanting to feel complete, when the real you is already complete and always was. Having once felt intense fear at reading statements like these, mind saying "you don't understand, I am completely alone, I feel I may die if I cut anyone out" - firstly, you're not as alone as mind thinks you are, and when you make the right choice for you, the right ones will flood the open spaces as quickly as you create them. Secondly, you are god experiencing a body, waiting for the right moment to show this to yourself. A few human beings less in your life will make zero impact on the you that you really are, and in fact if you are prepared to allow all past to dissolve in order to rise from the ashes, you will emerge no longer needing anyone or anything to be happy. This can be controversial, so I want to be clear here - as long as you identify as the human being, alone in the world, then your experience is going to conform to what psychology and medicine dictate based on observation of typical humans - you will need people. When you identify as the Infinite, you will no longer need people, and yet you will appreciate and love them as you never could as the needy, constructed human aspect.

### The Only Real Thing

In the introduction to "A Course in Miracles," a channeled

account of the path to liberation from suffering as received and written by clinical psychologist Helen Schucman, it says: "nothing real can be threatened. Nothing unreal exists." This sounds just cryptic enough that the mind can play it off as a non-literal statement you have no hope of understanding. The statement couldn't be truer, and it is literal. The one thing that sages and gurus have discovered over and over, independently of one another; the one thing all religion is based on; is that the world we are living in as human beings is a dream world with a beginning, an end, and a Divine purpose. It is not Consciousness, but it is *of* Consciousness. This Consciousness is so vast that it is capable of simultaneously operating the bodies of all humans - of breathing them into life. You didn't think your body could sustain itself, did you? Think about it - who is running your stomach? How are the multitude of chemical functions taking place in your digestive system, respiratory system, endocrine and nervous systems all at once? Who organized your self-healing body into a series of cooperative systems which, all things considered, typically function with incredible accuracy? Your mind is scarcely capable of rubbing the belly and patting the head at the same time, it certainly can't run the internal processes of the belly and head at the same time. Consciousness runs it, and runs all beings. It is simultaneously living all the lives that appear in what we call the world of form. When you hear this, your mind may automatically picture a big god in the sky, and that is certainly a way of viewing things based on concepts the mind has already become at least somewhat familiar with - however, when you let go of the idea that flawed humans of the past managed to sufficiently translate and communicate Divine messages without inserting their own confused notions; when you release all the ideas mind has associated with such a force, including releasing the meanings associated with the very words we use to describe it; when you allow the possibility that a force is governing all aspects of form and yet that force is completely without any attributes the human mind could conjure; you open yourself to experiencing it as it really is - because the same thing that is breathing all the bodies on earth is also the non-thing comprehending words, taking the garbled pictures from all eyes and giving them proper orientation and scale, and witnessing the events occurring everywhere. The body is the vehicle - it is not alive in itself. Consciousness is using an inert vessel with finite tools, breathing life into it for exactly as long as it wishes to, using it to observe its dream world. You have not lost your autonomy - you are That being, tricking yourself in a seamless virtual reality.

This can seem shocking - that the entire dream world was built by you in order to have experiences of what you are not - to enlist the services of the mind to convince yourself of the reality of the experience just to eventually let go of the mind. The dream is seamless precisely so that the dream can be so much fun to navigate - so real-feeling. But when Consciousness believes itself to be the bodymind unit it is observing, the small thoughts of mind have serious impact - we forget our power, the human functions in a destructive way, we buy into the thought that when something happens to the body it happens to us, and look for sources outside of ourself for a sense of relief from this dream. When we do this, the human experience becomes very limited - very unhappy. Because our true nature is happiness, and we have seemed to cut ourself off from the source of that happiness, that very thing begins to seem elusive and rather foreign. We look in vain for external sources to replace an ineffable happiness lost, and a true and unconditional source is not found until we drop the act.

If the mind is resistant to the idea that the world is an illusion, that is because the mind is a part of it. The mind is a part of the world of form, and cannot itself witness the Infinite. It would be like expecting your very normal non-autonomous vehicle to drive itself - it isn't equipped for that. Begin to move past the mind by constantly questioning elements of this dream world and of the mind itself until a space begins to form between you and the mind, making it obvious, unmistakable, that there is a me and an I. Then, reinforce the truth; that the thoughts aren't true.

One way I consistently questioned the dream world and the small identity called Heather was by focusing on the human propensity to dream. Isn't it interesting that when you begin to imagine yourself as the Creator of all things, you notice that humans are constantly dreaming, both awake and asleep? Notice how the mind possesses the capability of creating entire dream worlds, and when in sleep, we even believe they're real. Notice how in wakefulness, when something really wonderful happens, we tell others to pinch us to make sure it's real. Conversely, when something really bad happens, the mind itself stops wanting to subscribe to the dream it has created, and begins to dissociate - it tries to detach from the mindbody experience itself in order to escape pain. This attempting to escape pain is precisely the mechanism of the mind that causes our suffering, and in a state like this, the tendency is very strong. Why is it that human beings, the only beings we know of that are capable of thought, experience sanity like a tight rope walk or perhaps never at all? Why is it this hard? Because we are not the mind, and identifying with it is to make more and more real the flawed and finite - what we believe, we create, and we believe in false and harmful things.

When the illusion is seen through, you will cease believing you are the fictional character, and will play the character still knowing you are yourself, Awareness. Because this world is a game of energy, as you become less of the false, you become more of the true - less of what you are not, and more of what you are. Consciousness fills the gaps, and love becomes your identity. You no longer require success of any kind to be happy. You know that if you choose to have it you can, but you are happy without having it. It is this happiness that becomes a power that far exceeds the mind. Life opens up to you, and even the illusion you play with changes as you interact with it differently and put out a different energy. Your body cleans itself - dis-ease, except that which is a fixed condition to experience and accept in this lifetime, dissolves. The mind becomes a tool you can use at will, and even its power increases as it aligns with the Divine Will - the will of Consciousness, who you really are. As we drop the will of the personal, there will be an automatic realigning with what is completely natural and effortless - which, when you consider, must be the real you. Similarly, if the adherents of any faith began to place their faith in that which they truly are, away from the external - if individual energy was plugged into the reality that in each human experience is the capacity for goodness and realization of Divinity - all dogma would be rendered unnecessary. Life itself would be an effortless exercise in devotion, love, and inner stillness.

# CHAPTER SIX

## GROUNDWORK: COMING CLEAN

You know that friend you have who, when confronted with the consequences of their own conduct, will slither and squirm their way out of seeing it, using every excuse in the book? If only they would quiet down and listen, let down their defenses, they would see the obvious cause and effect being shown to them without injecting all sorts of other meanings into it - they would simply correct their beliefs and subsequent behaviors, and move on.

I'm sorry to be the one to break this news, but that is the mind. It is simply more prevalent in some than in others based on circumstance. Once again, this and so many other works would not be necessary if we simply experienced cleanly. As it is, when we attract dysfunctional relationships through our poor boundaries or low standards, the mind somehow still says the world is "doing this to us." When we despise our jobs and spend our days taking long breaks and gossiping, the mind thinks we deserve a better one than we have while our behaviors tell the world we have "more job than we can handle." While some situations do seem to just happen for some collective purpose, many are the result of the content of our minds and resultant behaviors. The message, as we've discussed, is so very simple - it is getting to a point of hearing it cleanly that can present a challenge.

In a world without chaos, where all is stable, one could simply realize the true self without fear, roadblocks, limitations, or side effects. As it is, humans are subject to what yogic philosophy refers to as the *gunas* - the three qualities of all things in the world of form.

*Rajas, tamas,* and *sattva* refer respectively to a slow, stagnant quality, a faster and more active quality, and the quality of consciousness, which is always in balance. The things we eat, the weather or temperature in the room, the qualities of the people around us, and the way we move our bodies are a few ways our human form is pulled in one direction or another throughout every day, and when you study yoga deeply, you learn to bring the body into sattva, or balance, more and more, until this is your permanent state. This can play a role in quieting the mind, at least enough so that when the truth is uttered, the spider web of thought seeming to block the light of Consciousness will be much less dense, allowing for the shifting of attention to the Divine that you really are.

When you begin to wake up from the illusion of the small self and realize yourself as the Infinite, the life circumstances you are currently experiencing will begin to shift. Sometimes when there has been significant trauma that has been left unresolved and therefore stored in the body, this can bring about significant side effects. Because of my experiences in life and my prolonged decisions to believe ideas that limited me, there was a great deal of suppressed emotion in the body which the ego used in an effort to keep the situation fearful and stagnant, clinging to a seemingly less scary status quo. This worked for a time and significantly delayed the process.

Despite the fear of going deeply into the process, suffering generated a strong will and I went through years of meditation and bodywork training, as well as received many bodywork sessions, and trained in yoga and coaching techniques. All these things prepared the small self to better withstand the process of realignment in the body. When there is strong attachment to the body and fear of every little thing that happens to and in it, there may be resistance to the unfolding process, as I experienced. It is important to acknowledge that this is completely okay. The process of awakening needs to be sustainable for you in order for you to continue with it. The ego wants to force through, but Awareness doesn't need to. In the end, the thing that will keep us on track is the recognition that all we are doing is releasing untruths - what can be dangerous about experiencing reality as it is, and what keeps us safe if the mental idea "reality is dangerous" prevents us from living? Reality is still reality, you're just avoiding knowing about it (spoiler: there's nothing to fear. Mind is just making a game of fearing reality).

In the Yoga Sutras of Patanjali, the very first verse says "and now begins the journey of yoga." The wider understanding of this simple statement is that once one chooses intentionally to "unite" with the Divine, and presumably if they have knowingly chosen to read The Sutras this will be the case, everything on one's path will begin to inform that journey. In my case, every time the mind tried to resist the path, decisions were made that were destructive enough to force the experience back into something of a humbled state, again open to the possibility that mind may not know everything. This helped the mind to recede, or for attention to more easily be diverted from it, and at that point, in a way, it was as if there was no choice. I was on the path, and Consciousness would show itself to itself within this lifetime, end of story.

Now is a fantastic time to realize the true self, because Western culture is more integrated than ever in holistic and "spiritual" aspects of wellness. More people than ever are undergoing yoga teacher training, during which they learn the deeper aspects of yoga and become familiar with the way energy flows in the body, the way different layers of the body interact with one another, and the true intention of the practice. As more people become aware of these aspects, we can begin to collectively support those undergoing awakening like never before. While this transition is currently being manifested as turbulence and chaos on the surface, it is making way for more authentic and organic experiences of becoming willing to go within for answers.

It is helpful to know at the beginning of this journey that not everyone is going to understand it, no matter how hard you try to explain it, and in fact it will be very helpful to protect your space and energy while attention on Awareness remains elusive or easily redirected. It is also helpful early on to drop any expectations of others coming along with you. Your awakening will serve as an example of happiness for those around you, but it is up to each individual to recognize a resonance with the Divinity on display or to resist it in favor of the play they are currently acting out and have become attached to. Many may not be receptive at first, and will have to find their own way to the path, at which time you can provide company and support if you wish. As you realize the Awareness that you are, those who are ready will come to you.

As the mind becomes purified and refined, you may relate less and less to the activities you used to do as well as people who do not support your journey. There may also be a time of limbo, where the old no longer fits and the new hasn't been recognized yet. My mind mistook this shift for depression at first, simply based on a belief behind these "symptoms." Realization of the true self means that you are realizing your sacredness; mistreatment will not bother you as it once did, and yet it will not be tolerated, and you may simply choose to allow relationships to dissolve when they show themselves to no longer serve your highest good and to be beyond conversation about it. A significant reason for delay on my journey was that I was not prepared to be without the people whose voices had become the abusive and dismissive ones in my mind - when there was no more clinging to the mind, there was no more clinging to that which had previously seemed to define me. Relationships that could easily crumble were allowed to, and those who showed the ability to grow with me, or at least to allow me to grow without resistance, became even closer. What's more, physical and emotional energy were no longer plugged into relationships which were a drain, and all the freed up energy allowed for greater mental clarity as well as the space to connect with those who were interested in knowingly being the love they already are.

## The Dream Wants You To Dream It

As Consciousness takes up more space in your experience, as you knowingly become more of yourself, you may find that life throws more challenges at you for a while. The game of form has all sorts of magnetic qualities, as it wants you to buy into it - it wants to draw you back in, to have your energy plugged into it. In this case, plugging in simply means to believe in it as the only reality. If the movie "The Matrix" came to mind at this, you're not that far off. You may unknowingly plug back into the game many times before you can harness attention enough to realize in the moment that you are doing it and unplug again. Throughout this process, remembering that you are love itself will allow you to access limitless self-compassion, giving grace to make mistakes without judgment - after all, engaging in judgment is acting as the mind, and adding energy to it. To finally observe the mind acting out its whims with an objective detachment, you will know you are there - and if you're like me, you'll laugh for days at the paltry attempts to reel you back into the game. Nothing can hurt you, so there is no need to make an enemy of the mind. You see it as a small thing, grasping and trying, and it becomes rather amusing, like watching a kitten unravel your knitting. "Ohhhh you cutie," you say to the mind that has had you engrossed for your entire lifetime. "You're just too much, yes you are." You see its innocence, and that it has not once affected the real you.

If you find yourself struggling with a shift in your relationships, this is where meditation and exercises in refining and purifying the mind can be helpful. Though meditation in the formal sense is not necessary to realize the true self, if the mind is so chaotic that you cannot even focus on the words in books or talks, or if resistance is so strong that your fear comes with considerable symptoms, there is a need to first ease the mind into a state where it is more receptive. This is something a coach or guide may help you to determine, or if you can access intuition at this time, you can determine this for yourself. If you feel you have to force the journey to make it happen, it will be well worth it to learn to be still and gentle with the small self before that self is ready to take on a paradigm shift.

On my journey, I did the work by myself. There was nobody in close proximity on such a journey that I knew of, and I had a limiting belief and fear that I had to do everything by myself, which is what brought about my isolating circumstances to begin with. When those beliefs were finally released, I found I encountered several people right away on a similar journey. Many people will experience something similar unless they place or find themselves near a community of "seekers" of whatever kind. In my case, it was for a reason and for the best - I was meant to overcome the feelings of loneliness which made it seem as though I was alone in the world if someone wasn't actively making demands on my time. Ultimately, while a coach and various books and recordings can help point you in the right direction, you will need to be able to reflect alone, to work it out alone. It is by design that we must work out our own liberation. Nobody can save a god who just needs to realize they are That.

**Nothing is Permanent**

As your mind begins to open to the possibility of cracks in the apparent reality of the dream world, as you entertain the idea that it may not be as solid as once believed, it will actually begin to resemble a less solid thing. Circumstances in your life may change rapidly - you may find that your job requires you to be completely subscribed to it - that it requires a level of buy-in to the system which you no longer have. From where you sit now, that might sound like too much trouble, too scary. I personally experienced so much change throughout my life that leaving a job was no longer scary - I'd done it a dozen times and it was not an unknown. For those who have come to depend upon and value supposed stability, it might seem quite negative when things fall apart. However, this falling apart is only taking place for things which are best left, and precisely when the Universe is shining its spotlight on your life, allowing for a more conscious rebuilding. The upset at a loss of job, relationship, money, or material things can inspire us to look at why we are so attached to the way things are in such a changing world, why the change upset us so. When we investigate this and identify our messengers - the feelings that tell us where our triggers are and where we need to work - we have laid out our path rather nicely. Applying mindfulness as you encounter this resistance, recognizing it as resistance and simply allowing it to be there without feeding it, is to entirely disrupt the process of resistance - you gently refuse to perpetuate it. When you notice the mind resisting, or even the body throwing up signs of resistance, just... stop... resisting. There isn't a way to "do" this - it is in non-doing that we achieve it. This can feel dangerous to the mind which has so self-importantly deemed itself "the only one who gets anything done around here," but the impermanent mind is often a hindrance rather than an asset when it is misused, and the space made when it steps aside allows Consciousness to flood in, running life much more efficiently, healthily, and effortlessly than the mind could ever achieve.

### Effortless Awareness

When I was a child, as part of the "Gifted and Talented" program within my school, we were required to deconstruct the aspects and parts of a poem. As a result of my personal experience with this, I lost all understanding of it as a pure form of art, and until recently I had no interest in hearing it read aloud. It seemed labored and overly dramatic, pointless - *if you want to say something, just say it clearly and openly!* was my opinion. Of course, in this way I was preventing myself from enjoying an accessible and vulnerable human activity, and only recently came to peace with this form of art through the compelling work of Rumi, and with the curious thought, *in what way would this life be different had I opened myself to poetry and poetry readings? Who would I have met, how would the work have touched my heart?*

As the non-judging ultimate Creator, all forms and levels of art are easily enjoyed. Similarly, judgment of others' performance in any area falls away when one is knowingly staying as their true nature. Because of this, we are uninhibited in our own forms of creation. Everything we do is done from a place of pure Knowing - there is no wrong, there is no hierarchy - we laugh at the hierarchy and all other forms of human folly. We laugh from love, because we know deeply the pain we ourselves have experienced and that it did not once touch the true self - no humans were truly harmed in the making of this movie.

Running a business from a place of wanting money may indeed deliver on your goal, but won't bring happiness, and your overall success will be limited. Trying to become a teacher of anything when you don't care about the content or the student will ensure your job is difficult. I spent years as a bodyworker, a facilitator of healing in others, and I struggled with burnout constantly because I was working way too hard during each session and worried about whether my clients were happy with my work. I was trying to force the tissue to release and open, I was trying to get clients to do wellness "homework" they didn't want to do, and the way I presented myself must have been hindered by my own stresses. If you've ever met someone who was completely present, exuding peace in their every movement and word, your thought is "I want whatever they're having!" If you have to force your life, you will not put out that energy, and when you put your attention on this, you will be able to tell. You have seen people force their lives as long as you've been experiencing a body, and you may have taken on this tendency without realizing it. Part of recognizing your true nature is softening, learning to force nothing at all, and recognizing true inspiration and intuition when it arises. You will not be able to mistake it when it comes, and you do not need to learn it. It occurs naturally when resistance ceases.

When Awareness effortlessly becomes the focal point, that won't escape your notice either. Where before you took in 10% of your surroundings based on what the mind was trained to perceive, and mind content filled the remaining 90% of your attention span, with attention placed on Awareness you will experience 100% of your surroundings without any of the emotional marring you've become accustomed to, and intentionally use the mind when it is required. This is not something that needs thinking about - you will never figure it out with the mind, and trying to will only be the mind acting out an old pattern. As though watching clouds floating through the sky, watch the thoughts in the mind, identifying each one as a thought that is unverifiable and not from you. Once you realize this on a deep and experiential level, all is ease.

**Beliefs - The Big Drain**

Bias in our experience, which we derive from beliefs based on our past experiences, can look like this:

You meet someone new who interests you as a potential partner. You exchange information, and you decide to be open and vulnerable - you send them a message telling them you had a great time meeting them and would love to get together soon. They respond hours later saying, "sounds good, I'm busy this weekend and next weekend, maybe the Tuesday after that?" You think to yourself, *if they were interested they would make time - why don't they explain their plans? Is this person ready to make room for another person in their life?* These are interesting questions for the mind, but should not be taken for the truth - they are mere speculation, and lead to suffering before anything at all is truly known. Instead of following this thread, notice which parts of the personality are compelled to find problems this quickly, to try to end something before it begins, are afraid of rejection from someone who cannot possibly know the real you. If you follow this line of questioning, you will arrive at unconsciously held beliefs - that you "should" have a partner, that this partner is a reflection of your self-worth, that an inability to secure one individual's excitement around you means anything at all about you, that someone replying to you hours later means anything more than the simple fact that they replied hours later. When you see this factually, you can approach a new relationship with the feeling, no matter what happens, *I know my worth and will be happy.* Ironically, this not caring is precisely what will attract a healthy partner, should that be in the cards.

You've just started a new job and within the first week, all sorts of stressful situations arise. In response to a particular crisis, a coworker says half-jokingly, "That's ABC Corporation for you!" From this, you get the impression this is not a place you want to work - that your time here will continue in the same way. While you are completely at liberty to quit your job for a new one, it is worth considering many things, including: do I know for a fact this company has a negative culture or could this one coworker have their own misperceptions? Is this something worth speaking to another coworker or management about, to better understand expectations of the position? Would I benefit from simply deferring judgment for later? Of course, you will know whether you work in a place where it is a good idea to do that - and if it's not, you may be answering your own question with that determination. All that is for you will be easy, and indeed this means that humanity will need to realize that any job which absolutely requires a lack of ease is not a suitable job for a human. Awakening certainly does not require you to change your job - but some choose to when they understand their worth.

When I was in the early stages of allowing awakening to unfold within the experience, I found it difficult to articulate that process clearly to others. I was discussing this process with a new friend as I was describing my personal history, and she said, "wow, with a history like that, I don't know how you did it." I said that I knew from this vantage point that all that had occurred in my life did so to make me uncomfortable enough to seek long and hard enough until this process had gained enough momentum to carry on to completion - without that level of suffering, it wouldn't have worked. I told her that I learned from all the times when I found myself alone dealing with a life crisis that humans actually don't need each other for this - when we can access the Divine within, we are tuned into everything else, one with it, whole, and complete. She immediately responded, "no, I'd go crazy without my family. Like absolutely insane. We need each other." What I had said had struck a nerve, to the extent that it wasn't listened to fully, and this was with someone who had read the works of many of the teachers who profess the very same sentiment. All this from a single belief - that we are separate, and therefore need to extract energy from others or to ascertain that they feel a certain way about us in order to keep the individual self going. Psychology and medicine show us from direct observation of human behavior that we need touch, affirmation, and belonging from others. In terms of the physics of the world of form, they are absolutely correct. When you realize your true identity and become that, you will not be subject to the psychological limitations and needs of humans. It doesn't make the relative truth of psychology any less true within context - it just downgrades it from universal to relative truth.

From these examples, it becomes easier to understand how our subtle and not-so-subtle beliefs have great impacts on our potential to grow, our enjoyment and ease in life, and the likelihood that we will have a meaningful interaction with someone whose values are different from ours. Beliefs run the show, and we now have more than ever. In order to make a new friend, they must love anime, disc golf, a lacto-ovo-vegetarian diet, and be in a similar place on their spiritual journey. Many of today's requirements on relationships didn't exist fifty years ago, and yet we consider them essential to the maintenance of our constructed selves. If our family hold different political beliefs, they are doomedly self-obsessed or hopelessly superior. The more concepts we introduce to life, the less we are living as the simple and pure Awareness that we are.

**Your Hurt Becomes Your Help**
When we seek the true self, it is easy to bring our human concepts with us - we deny or fixate on our pasts, we filter ourselves, and we believe the journey should culminate in being spared the pain of the human experience. With these practices, we are resisting the very way things are, and this is a pointless way to bring suffering about. Let's make the distinction right now between pain and suffering - as the Buddha said, pain is inevitable, suffering is optional. Animals are excellent teachers in this - when they experience pain, they simply experience it. They do not resist it or wish it different, they do not dwell on the thing which caused it - a small exception being the intelligent domesticated creatures that are beginning to take on some human anxieties and health issues. Animals living in healthy environments shake off the past, stretch the body open several times a day, release excess energy as soon as they feel the urge, and remain present by nature because thought is not occurring within them. However, the human experience is uniquely poised to be capable of thought as well as distinguishing between thought and the true nature of the one experiencing the human, making us free from thoughts whether they are occurring or not. While in practice this can seem like going backward from an evolutionary standpoint, it is decidedly forward-moving to retain the ability to think and yet to choose not to identify with or as it, and to do it only when needed. We will still experience pain in life, but we do not need to suffer as a result of it. Attachment to life going a certain way is the root cause of all suffering, and resistance to what we deem to be negative outcomes is one side of that coin. Releasing ideas of how mind thinks pain and

past should appear in our lives, we can begin to use these to our benefit - our pain teaches us to soften, our suffering teaches us when we are off track. When we suffer, or more accurately, when the experience is one of suffering, the human body brings about symptoms and sensations to alert us to it, and it is doing exactly what it is designed to do.

Because we are conditioned to believe that all good things come from hard work, we approach the journey as though it is filled with it. We strain and force, continuing to learn that this isn't "it," until eventually enough conditioning and tension are released from the system to allow for jumpstart moments resulting from a phenomenon called kundalini awakening. This can sometimes occur unexpectedly to someone who is not on any kind of journey, but typically this is arising because one has been diligent in the process of releasing what holds them back. In this process, energy which has been compressed at the base of the spine (this energy is compressed by the sheer force of preserving the identity - it has its own "gravitational pull" of sorts) is released, which is like life force energy surging through the body momentarily. In this time we receive what are like downloads, finding that greater wisdom and discernment is suddenly "just here." This can be partial and take place over several instances, or instantaneous.

Consciousness is infinite and the bodymind is finite; this process may also heal the body of long held dysfunction. Because of this, there can be a dramatic shift which includes temporary symptoms from headaches, shaking, and surges of energy to a sudden desire to make changes to life circumstances, emotional and sleep disturbances, and even what Western medicine deems to be temporary psychosis.

When you've gone through it, you can see this process simply as an entering of Consciousness into areas that haven't seen light for some time, a kind of shifting in the nervous system, and it is not uncomfortable in itself; healing can be messy, and the mind can be attached to the old way. It is the resistance to the unknown which brings about any prolonged experiences. Some of these symptoms could easily be grouped and classified as one dis-ease or other, and it is important in these instances to remember that dis-ease is simply a lack of ease in the body which has been given a specific name based on the symptoms presented - it's all trial and error, observation-based, and still very much subject to your beliefs around it. I do not mention this phenomenon because it is of great concern; it is because if we buy into the idea that it is bad or unnatural, we will cause *ourselves* difficulty on the form level.

The more you practice techniques which will help you to withstand change in the body without buying into false thoughts about those changes, the more you practice some form of meditation and gradual releasing, purifying, and disciplining the mind, the easier the bodymind will weather this jolt. I say this because many people who go through this kind of shift are not aware of what it is, believe it to be an illness, and end up with a diagnosis and a mind-numbing prescription sure to stifle the process before it can be completed. Keeping in mind that this can occur during an awakening process can save unnecessary anxiety around the symptoms themselves, preparing you to allow the process to continue to unfold.

If you experience this as you begin to awaken and you feel you want help making sense of it, you can seek the counsel of a professional who has been through this process, such as an integrative medical professional, a therapist who is trained in the area, or a spiritual guide. They can help you to discern between sensations if you have any doubt. In my own experience, my body experienced a great deal of unwinding through Myofascial Release bodywork, energy work, Progressive Muscle Relaxation, physical yoga practice including yoga nidra and yin yoga styles, and my own intense awareness-building exercises. I went into this process with a great deal of difficulty relinquishing control over what was occurring within the body and hypervigilance relating to health. Multiple times I began to experience what I deemed was Kundalini Syndrome, and I took space from the work I was doing at those times. Finally, when I was able to disidentify with the fear held in the bodymind, I was able to allow the experience to complete its cycle. Because of the way mind generated suffering, the end result was appealing enough that I kept at my practice despite the discomfort. In the end, when I relaxed, the process was gentler, easier, and even enjoyable.

### Excuses, Excuses

*I'm too poor to attend retreats, I'm a visual learner, I've been brought up this way and it's all I know, I'm too old to start something new, I'm not smart enough to understand these dense concepts, spiritual seekers and teachers annoy me.* I've heard it all in my own mind, from clients, and elsewhere so often that human resistance has revealed itself as comically formulaic.

The most wonderful news of all is that concepts do not need to be understood by the mind in order to awaken - all the concepts in this book are a form of deconstructing, only necessary because of the many roadblocks presented by the mind. Often a highly intelligent mind can seem a hindrance on a path of discovery of the self, at least at first, because one's idea of their own intelligence can limit curiosity and openness or cause one to place far too much faith in the mind. In this case a kind of humbling will need to occur, and as someone who experienced a great deal of pummeling before I was finally ready to see the mind wasn't "it," believe me - life will show you.

Finances can be a point of contention in how one sees their spiritual teacher, guide, coach, etc. and I've found that many use this as an opportunity to find fault and walk away. The mind is looking for corruption everywhere, and it will find and even perpetuate it.

What is often confused is that even when one is completely self-realized (better said: when a particular experience is of total realization), they still retain the ability to exist simultaneously as both the small self and the infinite self - they still have the option of playing whatever game with form that they choose. Their games will of course be more benign and effortless, but don't mistake it - fully realized individuals are not required to adhere to a Christian, Buddhist, or even human code of morality. Continuous knowing contact with the Divine creates its own kind of morality, better seen as inherent goodness, because we realize we are all one, so we will not hurt another. This new kind of morality or goodness is without any obligation or pressure, so what a mind thinks about one's conduct is inconsequential. These individuals have moved beyond the concepts of the mind, and when they engage in the Divine play of form, they can do whatever they like.

Because realization of the truth can be a process which continues to deepen over a lifetime, it may be that traces of an egoic self remain in a knowledgeable teacher with much to offer. A teacher who charges a great deal for a retreat, yet offers their collected works and a myriad of free courses or talks online, has given all they see need to give - they have fulfilled their mission in that. The rest is simply playing in the game of form, in which these teachers understand that nobody is truly suffering and all must ultimately liberate themselves. Putting one's understanding out into the world to be interpreted as it will is the highest good they can offer humanity. One teacher may have observed that when many students pay more for a retreat, they arrive more committed to welcoming a lasting change within themselves, and they can choose to play with that observation. What they choose to do with money that has flowed to them as a result of their writing has no effect on you - do not allow the small self of another to derail you on your journey to the greater self right in front of you, within you.

Once you see yourself as the shining light that you are and understand the world of form for what it is, you will know without a doubt that there is no valid reason to remain in unhappiness, an emotion meant solely to alert us to our having lost sight of ourself. Notice the mind judging the messenger, limiting your options, and placing conditions upon happiness - then let that go.

## Mind - the Furthest Thing from True

It's time to face the truth - and the thoughts in the mind are not that. The few things that could be considered completely true about life on this planet might not be true in another dimension or outside of the limits of perception, and while it can be easy to ignore a dimension the human eyes and ears cannot detect, they are still there. If you are truly seeking after the Truth, it is Universal Truth you want - and that includes not one single thought of the finite mind. Human intelligence is a part of the mask, the constructed identity, and the more attachment there is to the way the mind says things are, the more challenging it may be to relinquish an identity centered around it. The goal is to unlearn, or release, knowledge which boxes in the experience and narrows the view.

The way that we want to begin to see the mind is as a tool for our experience on earth - it executes tasks. Awareness is able to understand everything that unfolds perfectly - thoughts are not required to have a full experience, and are much like watching a movie with commentary on - you're missing half the movie trying to listen to it. Awareness created machines with which to experience a life on earth. These bodies are equipped with minds that can be quite powerful in their earth functions - when we believe the thoughts, our reality looks like the thoughts. This is a built-in part of the earth game. When there is a belief in thought, we are making them true in more ways than one. When you can use the mind to intentionally create the world you want and put it aside the remainder of the time, you begin to use the mind as the ultimate creative tool, rather than letting it use and perpetuate itself and confusing its voice as the real you.

You have heard the voice of the mind since you were a small child.

You have listened to it since that time and everyone around you has told you it is you. You even rebelled against this as a child, wanting to create your own reality but finding you were subject to others' beliefs. By the time you reach an age of understanding, you've already been indoctrinated into this understanding. What it is you are engaging in now is an intentional deconstruction (construct removal) of the mind - releasing the beliefs you've held onto and coming into a deeper Knowing that is indisputable. When I discovered nonduality as a concept, my mind rebelled quite strongly because it sensed a danger to its power and status. There was intense fear because of the extent to which I believed my entire being was encompassed in the mind - it seemed I was engaged in something very dangerous. All of these were false thoughts perpetuated by the mind and entirely supported by society.

These days, I see it as I would a child, and it becomes quite funny. When a child spills their soup and they seem to believe their world is over, and you as an adult can see that absolutely nothing is wrong (unless you've bought into the idea that spilled soup is a personal failing) - this is the feeling you get as you rise in understanding, able to see those around you suffering needlessly but knowing that their deeper Self, the same Self that you are, does not suffer and never will. We are whole and complete, acting out lives of desperation and suffering yet free to walk away from it at any time merely with a choice that is always ours to make. It's like a world full of gods wearing VR headsets and believing themselves to be engaging in Live Action Role Play, hitting each other with digital foam weapons and really believing themselves to be hurt - it's funny because nobody is being hurt! There is not a morsel of universal truth to the filtered images they see.

**Still Believe You Are Your Mind?**

If, like me, you have a strong attachment to and investment in the mind as your sole reality, the mind itself will place many roadblocks in the way of realization of the true self. With a little unbiased attention, however, those roadblocks will soon become just as amusing as the rest of its antics. First, it is important to look closely at the process of thought - can *you* turn it off? Or does thought occur without your sign-off? If it occurs when *you* don't want it to, who is the it, and who is the you? In this case, with *it* thinking and *you* becoming annoyed at not being able to turn it off, neither one is you - the real you is the one noticing the drama unfold, noticing two aspects to a hodge-podge identity having a fight between themselves. You are the objective observer of all things, and you never once leave your state of peace. When your mind is on a chaotic rampage and saying all manner of things to captivate your attention, who is instantly noticing that the mind is doing this? Who remembers your dreams when the bodymind is deep in sleep? Who is it that grabs the falling glass before it hits the floor when you know full well the mind cannot think that quickly? Who is it within the mother who picks up a car to save her child, when the car far outweighs the mother's supposed capacity to lift? Glaring signs present themselves as "miracles" in our daily lives, and yet we maintain that it is some far off mystery. It is in the releasing of the mind's limitations, which is only done when thought is suspended or disbelieved through disidentification, that the mind-made limitations on the body are also released, as the mindbody unit functions harmoniously.

More evidence: have *you* ever said something embarrassing or damaging to yourself? If *you* know it is embarrassing or damaging, why was your mind thinking it and your mouth saying it when it doesn't serve you? When *you* spoke rashly and hurt someone you loved, who was the *you* that chose to hurt another, and subsequently yourself, out of a sense of having been slighted or wronged? What part of you is acting without the consent of *you* based on an automatic response to seemingly being wronged? When you begin to pay attention to your thoughts and you notice them happening as they happen - who notices? Awareness, Consciousness, The Force, the unchanging and stable background that is dreaming this world into reality and lives all the lives it creates. You.

When you notice resistance or disagreement in the mind, it's easy to confuse one as the mind and one as you. The mind is capable of maintaining separate and differing aspects, and as it is a machine which takes on the values around it and it has found itself in spaces of conflicting values over time, different aspects of it take different positions. This is all distinct from Pure Awareness, because Awareness doesn't believe - it Knows. When attention is on Awareness, there is no doubt of anything, no fear. When fear is experienced objectively, we begin to recognize that it is happening, and we are watching it happen. We begin to realize we are not the fear, it is not real in an ultimate sense, and it no longer serves us as our primary focus. We release the fear, and yet we are still here - the fear was never a part of the real You to be lost. It was simply a passing feeling which captivated the attention of You so continuously that the experience of it has seemed to be You.

### The Reinforcers

There are many aspects of the life of form which are completely in the service of keeping attention captivated by the mind. Social media and television of any kind were created to tell stories, and many of those stories have agendas - subtle missions to leave behind a message, an imprint on the values of society. Any television show will seek to reinforce one's idea that they are a small self, that the stories they perpetuate are real, and that they hold weight and importance. Watching lovers go through dramatic breakups on television, the mind believes that to be broken up with is an incredible shame, a slight on the individual which requires binge eating, hours of deconstruction with friends, or a mental breakdown. In reality, dropping these ideas of the self will allow the self to recede - we become aware that others' choices have nothing to do with us, that we are whole and complete in a way the mind cannot even comprehend and that is an untouchable truth.

I was addicted to social media for years after going through a divorce. That person had seemed to complete me, and without him, I needed to find the missing puzzle piece. I had done enough work on the self to realize that I did not want to compromise my values, and yet I searched and searched in places where I was highly unlikely to meet a compatible match, therefore subjecting myself to a great deal of unnecessary heartache, disappointment, and unreciprocated energy expenditure. It felt as though I was burnt out at the soul level, my heart emptying day by day. With a social network of people generally too busy or not interested enough to cultivate deep friendships, I looked to social media to fill the gap, and I began to check for connection opportunities many times a day.

When I finally realized all of this, it became rather easy to release social media. I deleted any presence of it from my phone and left it that way for months. I noticed that nobody realized I was gone; I also realized that I didn't care, and that this process made it quite easy to start fresh with friends who recognized my absence. I did not need them to, as this whole process had taught me to be complete within the higher self. It was a standard I felt I could not walk back from. I learned at last that the experiences I was having were the result of decisions, and I could decide differently.

### The Bodymind - A Deeper Look

During my training as a yoga teacher, I was quite interested in the teachings of the koshas - the overlapping layers of the body which we can experience distinctly from one another, but which all have an effect on each other.

To understand this, we must recognize the physical body to be what quantum physics has confirmed - ultimately, only waves of energy dependent upon Consciousness to take a certain form. Most people, even those with a loose or begrudging understanding that the body is not solid, retain their existing beliefs about the physical body as distinct - that the different parts have distinct borders, that the mind and its thoughts exist in the brain, and that the emotions go right along with a thought. However, when you understand that the body is capable of hanging onto the results of emotions in the energetic layer, that thoughts are occurring non-physically and the brain is simply lighting up as a physical response to the thoughts, and that these thoughts and emotions affect how the physical body appears and functions, then the idea of the body as layers begins to make sense. I like to think of these layers as taking up the same physical space but operating in different dimensions.

The five layers of the body are, in English and in Sanskrit:

The physical layer - Anamaya kosha
The energetic layer - Pranamaya kosha
The mental layer - Manomaya kosha
The wisdom/intuition layer - Vijnanamaya kosha
The bliss layer - Anandamaya kosha

Typically, the human experience is mainly comprised of the workings in the physical, energetic, and mental layers of the body. Working inward, each layer becomes subtler and requires more of our attention to experience it knowingly. In order to experience wisdom and bliss, we must begin to purify these "outer" layers and allow that reality exists beyond them. When the physical body has blockages, it affects our ability to experience the mind in a clean way. When the mind contains debris of false beliefs and takes up all the available space of attention, it clouds the view of intuition. When we are able to move past the mind, we can experience wisdom, and wisdom leads us to bliss.

It is important to note once again that there is most certainly the possibility of awakening fully, or of realizing one's true nature, without understanding the layers of the body, practicing yoga, or meditating. The indirect path, that of gradually purifying the experience and preparing the nervous system to withstand a physical transformation which occurs as identification with the human is released, includes daily rituals and can include locating supportive communities. The direct path, practiced more in recent years, I simply do not recommend on its own for those experiencing particularly great mental resistance or lack of support. In fact, for most I suggest the compassionate path, taking things gradually while also allowing and opening to instances of great revelation and shifts in understanding beyond what the mind is capable of.

This information is specifically for those who wish to purify their experience as the small self in order to help the process along, or to allow any sensations the body may present upon realization to be integrated more gently. For those who may notice a great deal of resistance to the truth, that they are the Infinite being watching a human experience play out, the practices of yoga and meditation as well as working through the koshas to experience more wisdom will be quite valuable. No need to overthink this - going beyond the apparent aspects of the bodymind allows intuition and wisdom to come in. We do not need to introduce a highly technical sense of this unfolding.

During my experience as a massage therapist, while I was not successfully cultivating much acceptance of the present moment, I was immersed in the practice of increasing awareness of the present moment through the deep and somewhat repetitive practice of bodywork. In gaining laser focus on what was happening in a client's physical body and energy field, feeling highly confident in my work and moving beyond the mind to trust my instincts, intuition arose when I was not even aware that I was working toward that end. However, this intuition has limited applications without an understanding of it. While I was able to trust my intuition a great deal in my work, it did not even extend to my other business practices, let alone to my personal relationships or my thoughts, to a great extent. Ernest Hemingway had wonderful insights on life and was able to write with a rare clarity and confidence. He is noted as speaking eloquently about embodying the present moment. This did not prevent him from destroying relationships and damaging his body with his many habits. Many artists are able to enter a flow state which allows them to create works that speak to the creator, to the Divine within other humans. This clarity may not extend to their personal lives if they carry erroneous beliefs in other areas of life which cloud their understanding. Spiritual teachers who have studied their subject matter for a lifetime have been implicated in abuse scandals or experienced addiction and suffering, despite being quite influential in positive ways outwardly. The mind is capable of creating doubt and discord even in the cases of the most practiced and fervent individuals. What must be realized for intuition to apply to all of life's circumstances is that the beliefs of the mind are not true, are not a reflection of the true self, and the only universal truth is that we are all ultimately the same Divine being, living out all lives on the planet and beyond. When we realize in our bones that all form is a dream, we drop all illusions surrounding that dream, and we knowingly experience the joy and peace befitting the dream for the first time.

# CHAPTER SEVEN

## THE ULTIMATE SURRENDER

**What Does It Mean To Surrender?**

As we discovered earlier in this book, there are no perfect words when it comes to the Infinite. Words will always fall short, and it's up to us to learn the intended meaning between them by hearing cleanly with an earnest desire to understand truth, rather than filling in blanks with convenient answers. Another way to say this is to listen with the heart. A great example of a concept that is often misunderstood is surrender. When we hear this, we often imagine ourselves defeated, giving up on life, or saying it's okay to have life go terribly, we will do nothing to stop it. In fact, to surrender is not to give up on life at all - it is to cease going through life as the powerless small self, trying to force things to happen that are outside of our control, believing that mind and body will get things done.

To surrender is not to be defeated; rather, it is to recognize the limits of the mind and realize that nothing needs forced. It is to realize that the mind has done its best, but that best is just about nothing compared to what the Higher Self, Awareness, or Consciousness can do. This is rather paradoxical; it requires us to drop the small self and yet bask in the glory of the true Self. Not for a second do you need to feel worthless or that you are surrendering to an outside god because you do not possess any redeeming abilities. In "humbling" the small self, in realizing that Divine Will has been running the show the entire time and the small self has been resisting that; when this resonates deeply, there is a freedom and a joyful curiosity to see how life will go when the will of the small self is aligned with the Divine's - it is aligned because the supposed will of the small self is let go of, and life is allowed to unfold however it chooses. Basically, you are the Divine, finally acting like it - you are navigating an illusion without getting sucked into it. You know that all is ultimately well, that this is a dream, that you as Consciousness itself cannot be touched and do not die - and with this, all of life becomes your playground. By becoming less of what you are not, you see that who you really are will naturally take up more space. In that, there was never anything to seek - it was there, beneath the false.

### Have You Suffered Enough Yet?

Over the years, as this journey has evolved, I am asked more and more often what people can do to overcome the immense suffering in their lives. Because I was still working from a misguided view, trying to force things through for the happiness of Heather, and trying to help people rather than letting them help themselves, both the people I attracted and the way I answered these questions would ultimately result in each person reacting as if to say, "cool idea, but life isn't that hard yet. I'll come back later."

Having learned the futility of doing the work for another, I ask you this: have you suffered enough to be willing to drop every single tiny thing which no longer serves you, even down to the identity you have contrived along the way? This hard-hitting and perhaps elusive question is an important one to continue to ask yourself as you begin or carry on. When you notice that a message "seems like it should resonate" but doesn't, can you identify the part of you that isn't ready to let it sink deeply? Where is the repression, and is it pervasive? When you find that you're still attracted to people, things, and situations that bring chaos to your life, can you identify the part of you interested in attaching to something unhealthy or ignoring the signs, and perhaps overlooking that which is quietly better for you?

The following are just some of the requirements of a student seeking to enter into an immersive meditation program or a traditional yoga training program.

*Students must:*
*Approach the course material with the utmost reverence*
*Maintain a humble and open mind, offering maximum opportunity to take in the intended meaning of sometimes dense material*

*Refrain from any disparaging behavior toward the teacher and fellow students - avoiding at all costs any engagement in conflict*

*Refrain from any complaining, criticizing, blaming, negative, stubborn, egoic, dishonest, lazy, lethargic, or insensitive behaviors*

*Think only positively about oneself, refraining from any disparaging comments about one's body, mind, or speech*

*Show respect and gratitude for all teachings, even when confusion or disagreement exists within the mind*

*Keep up a dedicated daily practice, recognizing that to cleanse what the mind has taken on over decades, we must expect to invest time and resources to this end*

*Take well to criticism and other feedback, understanding that a message that is difficult to take in or elicits a strong response is showing exactly where one needs to contemplate and heal*

So - are you ready to approach your own awakening with this kind of humility, or are you pushing away teachers with distrust and intellectual critique? There is, as always, no blame in this - if you find yourself in this place, the small self is simply acting out effects of causal things that have happened in this lifetime. The more that has happened, the more we say "I can't be expected to let go of all this in favor of some fantastical and elusive peace." And sure - by earthly, human standards there is no reason to expect a put-upon human to do anything other than opt for what the mind deems the path of least resistance, whatever way that doesn't require excavation into the dark recesses of the small self.

I find it extremely instructive and accountability-building to begin to notice when the mind is acting out not being humble in my journey - when there is an allowing of the small details to mire the deeper message, enjoying one teacher but finding that another has a voice, style, or message I judge to be less than or which triggers a bias based on fuzzy memories. While these triggers and judgments are not my fault, as the small self is just acting out cause and effect with the tools it's been given, they are my responsibility to transcend and discern around.

We have one shot - in this bodymind, this time around. When we come back into the game, we come in with a different karma, a different life situation, and perhaps into a society which is less amenable to realization than the present one, not to mention the fact that we will come in with amnesia once again and will be lucky to retrieve any knowledge whatsoever of a "past life," which will depend a great deal on our even encountering the circumstances favorable to our believing in said past lives. With this one shot, are you ready to endure temporary discomfort in realizing that your belief in the mind as you has been the only thing seemingly separating you from peace? Are you ready to recognize where you have shut people out from an unwillingness to be accountable for your own actions, have sabotaged yourself or relationships, caused pain to yourself and others? If not, that is okay, that is the karma being experienced within this lifetime. Your journey will certainly continue, and ultimately, realization of the truth is always possible. However, even on a dedicated journey, when we decide to get hung up on the details rather than the intent of the teaching, we are delaying our own liberation - the mind, with its learned opinions, is running the show.

The saying "when the student is ready, the teacher will appear" has played over and over in my life in the past decade. I have noticed without fail that when my behavior changes, it aligns my life with different people, behaviors, lessons, and challenges. When I sat at home scrolling on my phone, attempting to date from a pool of other people who choose to date that way, and habitually ducked out of opportunities to build real community, only investing in my wellness secondarily through bodywork trainings out of state, I was amassing a small group of completely disjointed out-of-state friends, many passive male acquaintances, and spending money on drinks or food I didn't want rather than on yoga. When I shifted my priorities, I met people capable of supporting my journey, no longer felt regret about the way I spent my evenings, and as a wonderful side effect, felt myself loving where I lived more than ever before. In addition to this, I began to enjoy solitude as more than simply passing the time until I had the energy to be around people again - my inner world softened and deepened so that it was lovely to spend time there. Despite all the excuses I deemed myself justified in using, somehow new life circumstances were created from just a few changed behaviors.

When we believe the statement to be a mystical one and this journey to be a far off spiritual experience, with any inner change seeming to be outside of our control and somehow dependent upon outer circumstances, we are missing our teachers daily. At the start of our journey, if and when we are surrounded by those who are not prepared to support positive change in us, we are supplied with un-teachers of the very best sort. The moment we choose to intentionally engage in the journey of realization of our own Divine nature, everything around us is now in service of that goal. If the mind thinks it's agreed to the journey but cannot grasp what needs to be let go of, we will continue to resist the very best the Universe can give - examples of what not to do, what to transcend, the thoughts that hurt to buy into, what to release to make room for that which serves us.

Early in my journey, when I began to embrace yoga as more than a workout and occurring in more places than just the synthetic mat in my spare bedroom, when I decided I wanted to help people, and dabbled in Buddhist concepts, I experienced subtle resistance from those around me in the form of seemingly good-natured ridicule. Over time, there was a palpable difference. The more I made non-traditional decisions, the more there were implied statements and actions around my having failed in conventional terms, even though I experienced relative ease and consistency and was building loving and honest relationships. However, I retained beliefs I had internalized early on about my being strange, other than, difficult, too analytical, a quitter (as if that were a bad thing), and undeserving of what I had and the people around me. In some ways these beliefs were perpetuated through my actions, and they seemed to be reflected even in the sentiments of the new people I met. Because of this, it took quite a long time for me to realize incredibly obvious things - I would be happier without proximity to this criticism, I deserved to be treated with love, others actually liked me, and the more I engaged in the world the more I met these others. In all the time that I ignored these facts, I experienced a constant low level of anxiety, near-breakdowns over what I can now describe as "not terribly much, really," identity crises, burnout, and a lack of confidence that I could do anything to change my circumstances. After a period of intense loneliness during the isolation of 2020, followed by a rash decision to enter and seemingly entrap myself in an unhealthy romantic relationship, suddenly a great deal was on the line. Finally, in the decisive and swift dissolution of that relationship, in living alone once again and experiencing the peace that came with the way I chose to manage my own life, in embracing solitude rather than lamenting loneliness, I realized: I could completely transform my life simply through investment in what I already cared about, and in dropping any concern whatsoever for how this would affect the way others saw me - in other words, in dropping the mind and following intuition, the higher self. This led to the major breakthroughs that would become the realization of my true nature and that of every being - my suffering became my healing when I had finally suffered enough to face it and use it.

When I reflect on the hard-headedness I began with, the propensity to avoid uncomfortable situations, the tendency to zoom in on the things I didn't like about teachers who offered inconvenient lessons - all without for one minute checking myself, I began to understand that until that point, the character of Heather had been simultaneously playing all the parts in a Universal play of cause and effect going on in the head. Now "I," the true I of Awareness, was knowingly beginning to grab the reins. The god who had been willingly tricked by itself into believing in a dream world was recognizing itself.

If you have quit meditating after one class, saying you're "just not someone who can meditate," then what you say is true. If you believe yourself not ready to realize the truth, you are not. After years dancing around the edges of different lessons of all sorts, in retrospect it is clear that certain words or concepts, simply through their foreign nature, seemed out of my grasp. It was that thought, not any real limitation, which hindered and delayed the journey until the small self had been shown over and over and over - "you're not it." Having finally surrendered and embraced knowing that I don't know, real Knowing flooded in. Once again, there is nothing esoteric in this message. A simple and actual shift in focus, from the mind and things to the stillness and space behind things, was all it took for a journey of a lifetime to come to an end in weeks. You must believe this is true for you, and you must believe that the end to your suffering will be worth discomfort of the unknown. Only when the goal outweighs the fear of pain will you become willing to sacrifice the things that have kept you complacent, and only you are capable of working out your own liberation.

It might seem that to realize you were the one who set your own trap this entire time would result in a pain too great to bear. There was a time when I feared the bad feelings of accountability so much that I simply lied to myself, and you can imagine how my journey progressed under those circumstances. Over years of slowly recognizing the judgmental part of the mind, simply noticing it and moving on, that judge became a lot quieter. By the time I realized just how much the mind had delayed realization of the truth, I no longer heard the voice in my head that would say "you idiot! How could you have done this!" Instead, these epiphanies came with elation, lightness, and freedom. Actually, it was and is hilarious. To recognize your own part in your suffering and to instantly feel joy is to experience the love that you truly are - all judgment and resistance is just further mind content.

### When the Student Is Ready...

Can you think of any potential teachers along your journey who you missed through your own self-imposed limitations? Maybe there was a high school math teacher who told you you were capable of so much more than your C- grades. Maybe your mother told you you just need to allow people to love you. Maybe you went to a meditation retreat and gravitated toward the "bad kids" in class, finding the fervent students intimidating or boring, or noticing one egoic aspect of them and yucking the whole premise. Or maybe your teacher is right in front of you - the therapist or coach telling you session after session that you are worthy of love, or telling you precisely how to release destructive thoughts and behaviors, and yet the mind's programming can't help but assail you night and day with images of your parents telling you you were jealous of your siblings or difficult to raise. Maybe you see a massage therapist monthly, and after the session you zone out when they explain to you what might help you between sessions - after all, you're paying them to fix you, you shouldn't have to do anything. Recognizing these missed opportunities is key to beginning to use what you already have.

### Thy Will Be Done

I have realized over the years that the Christianity I was indoctrinated into actually bears striking similarity to other religions and philosophies, and the things which divide them are really of little consequence and easily reconciled. We have discovered that the original meaning and intention of the word sin is "missing the mark," or being untrue to oneself - there was no moral affiliation to the word or concept originally. When one shifts their understanding of sin and rereads the Bible, quite a different feeling and message are derived. Instead of a sky god sending down punishment when sin occurs or keeping a tally, we are left with a better understanding of *karma* - not a tally sheet which determines which creature we will be reborn as, but a flow of cause and effect, a shift in how the dream of life treats our form-based projections based on the lessons we still need to learn, as evidenced by our buy-in to illusory ideas. And one need not fear their thoughts, afraid that this vengeful god will bring down punishment when even the thoughts are out of order, a dizzying prospect that had me living in fear as a teen - we've come to understand that thoughts are just a function of the mind, the process we use when we assume a physical human body on earth which will, overall, determine the experience we have internally. And finally, we have no reason to fear a god that is separate from us because we are that god - each of us a package of the Consciousness which creates and lives all lives, and ultimately anything but plural. When we come to understand Jesus as an enlightened being whose mission was to bring the good news, that each of us is living in a hell created by the mind, by sin, and that we may simply walk away from it and live in Grace, in alignment with the will of god, our higher self - we begin to understand just how anyone in their right mind can believe "it is well with my soul." We are coming to find that everything we thought was scary and unbearable about this life is only a part of the dream, a lens we see through, and optional.

As such, I have finally come to embrace the phrase "thy will be done" for the first time in this life, having walked away from any dogmatic offerings and understanding the mission of the soul experiencing the body we call Jesus. I understand that a religiously affiliated person may see this as derogatory, arrogant, or egoic. I am not basing this on anything this mind has taken on, also known as beliefs, but on the unmistakable Knowing that has come from the mind's surrender. When the mind surrenders, when ego subsides, a state is revealed which is available to all who are willing to investigate this openly and fervently. It will, however, not be provable outside of the display of one's own peace in the illusion, and the more attached one is to the mind the more they will find this rather benign message upsetting. That is the irony and beauty of this world, which resembles the exact opposite of the formless, timeless, judgment-less non-thing that is the only actual truth. It's funny. It's so funny, so loving, so welcoming, that there is no room for concern for the reception of this imperfect work, completed in conjunction with Awareness and this finite mind. Knowing identification with the Infinite has made the mind recede, and left in its place a state which is much more peaceful and unshakable. It is not personal, because there is no person, and there is now a Knowing that it never was.

The prevailing understanding of the phrase "thy will be done" is to submit to a god outside of us. The nondualistic use of the prayer, in which there is no separation between god and things because all things are projections of god, is to relinquish the human aspect of the self, to understand that that which is truly important cannot be known by the mind, and one will function optimally without the interference of that mind. The Christian idea of dying to the self is the same as that of spiritual teachers, to "die" to the world before the body expires. In this, we relinquish the churning efforts of the mind and allow the small self to recede, no longer feeding it, yet having access to a cleaner mind mechanism anytime one wishes. In living this way, one aligns their life with the Will of the one who is orchestrating this life dream, and so no longer resists that which has occurred and is occurring. One no longer tries to control that which will occur, which leaves ample space for the "peace which passes understanding" to flood in. This peace, described in Christianity, can be felt by anyone who simply sits in front of a tree and observes it just as it is, without judgment or commentary, allowing it to be just so and noticing it with the curiosity of a child. To observe without the mind is an art form in itself, and to begin to practice this in daily life brings about a natural inclination toward submitting to the will of the Universe - because it's going to happen anyway, and it is ultimately you doing it, and every aspect of it serves the smaller self either through joy or the opportunity to release that which is not joy. When this lesson is learned, life opens up - there is no further reason to refine the mind, no lessons needing learned, nobody needing to be forgiven - one is knowingly living as Consciousness, and the most basic misunderstanding of humanity has been corrected.

To live in this way, one welcomes the rain falling upon them. One welcomes experiences in the place where they live and with the people they know, and when it is determined through inspiration and intuition that one desires to move, they simply move. There is no waffling, no indecision, no urge or pull to escape what currently is. When one finds that a person in their life is taking offense to the new boundaries being practiced as one learns to love oneself (actually, to realize one is the source of all love and allow it to flow), they know from a place of love that it is time to simply allow it to dissolve in the light of love, and they do so in a loving way. When the surface of one's life seems to be falling apart, one is aware in each moment that all of this is occurring for their highest good, is happening for them rather than to them. In this way, decisions are always inspired, even when there is a seemingly negative outcome; one weathers discomfort without any disturbance to the quiet peace one experiences within. This is the ultimate honoring of God, the true self. When you honor and do not resist, there is alignment with reality.

Any time you recognize that you are doing the dishes but wishing them already done, you can realize that you are resisting an inevitable thing, and that this is rooted in the mind. When you notice this resisting, there is the tendency then to resist the resistance - one can spend years in this state, absolutely forlorn at the way the mind works and one's apparent inability to curb or stop it. This is the mind feeding itself through more and more content, more focus, more attention placed on it and not on the changeless, peaceful background that you are. And who is it that is observing the mind? You are. Realizing this and finally stopping the feed of energy into the thoughts, to simply watch them pass by without hooking into them, is to stop the flow of resistance - and when there is no resistance, the situation cannot continue to perpetuate itself. By doing the one thing that makes no human sense, to allow something "bad" to exist in that moment, one experiences peace, and soon after follows lasting happiness - heaven on earth.

Soon after leaving the unhealthy relationship which had seemingly required all my time and energy to navigate minefields of emotional triggers, I bought and moved into my own house. This house, situated in a comfortable neighborhood with varied and easy-going neighbors, was the perfect size for my cat and me, easy to maintain, and I could afford it for a while even without a job, a state of ease which would allow me to finally place my attention on what needed to be acknowledged within. The dream I had conjured years prior was coming true, and I was elated, albeit burnt out and recovering from the situation I had just left.

The Friday after I moved in, the house across the street was hosting a party with guests continually coming and going, so much so that neighbors could not even get down the street or park in front of their houses. This party carried on into the night, noisy and concerning to more than me. I found out the next day that this house was a short-term rental and it was something the neighbors just felt they had to put up with, but not without continual calls to the police and arguments with the homeowner, an out-of-state corporation.

To my mind this was an insurmountable problem and a

continuation of some kind of curse of disruption following me around. This went on three weeks in a row, with neighbors up and down the street simply standing on their porches watching. Police were called by neighbors several times, but they never approached the house or the partygoers.

My mind went all sorts of places trying to determine how to fix this, including selling the house I had just bought. One passing idea was a fantasy of having my arborist cut down all their trees. You know, to be nice. Finally, when I noticed this train of thought and redirected it to Awareness, I decided I would let it go. I had learned that resistance holds what we call problems to us, and that to release something from the mind is to learn the lesson, to stop resisting what is. I was amazed at how this felt when it occurred - I had dropped resistance to a life circumstance, and it was made of freedom. I knew that even if this issue did persist, I would be at peace, happy.

The next morning, as soon as I went outside, I was approached by my neighbor, and she was excited to share the news - her ongoing research had finally produced a result. The house across the street had been removed from the rental website.

I realized just after we finished speaking that I had received this excellent news in the first possible moment after releasing it completely from the mind - the moment I had emerged from my home, my neighbor had happened to be outside, and had happened to have checked the rental site that morning. It all seemed quite a coincidence if it had been one, and I realized the rapidity with which the story had changed.

Soon after this, having started a job at a city recreation center, a pre-teen girl enrolled in the summer day camp program at the center experienced an intense bout of "spiritual unconsciousness" - having been hit in the head with a ball during gym time, she suddenly went into a state of anger so all-consuming that she was not in control of herself. She began chasing after a fellow camper with scissors threatening to attack him, pushing me as well as other staff members with surprising force in the process and requiring four men to hold her down as she failed at a surprising number of attempts to bite and kick them. When her mother arrived, she began to interrogate staff including me, refusing to walk away when it was explained that we needed space to process what had happened.

That day, it was as though a decision had been made for me by a force greater than me - I knew when I went to lunch that I would not return, clocking out and leaving my ID badge and keys at the front desk for coworkers to find.

Aside from post-adrenaline rush shakes, I was at peace, and I knew that I had made the right choice and did not feel the fear of joblessness as I had done for most of my life to that point. I knew that all would be well. I woke up the next morning, experienced absolute freedom, empowerment, and joy - and knew that I must write. I sat down and wrote several thousand words in the next two days, continuing to write each day after that without any doubt that this was how I wanted to spend the coming days.

Halfway through, I knew this work would benefit someone just like me who wasn't quite ready to open to the awakening process. Almost finished, I had no desire to rewrite it as I had done so many times. I knew that this was the way I wanted to live, and that this was coming from the highest authority - the true self, Awareness. This was the will of Awareness - "thy" will was being done, and Heather was acting it out. As soon as I finished writing, I received a call from a recruiter looking to hire me at her company's headquarters, only a few miles from my new home, with the best pay and most engaging management team I had ever encountered in an interview process. The best part: they welcomed their employees to pursue supplemental work and outside activities, rather than requiring a false pretense of living for the company. After almost two decades of being unable to secure a role like that, suddenly this company was seeking me out, and I had gone from a life in pieces to the best circumstances yet in a matter of weeks. What's more, I acknowledged it all with a gratitude I had never been able to muster as only Heather - years prior, I may have had acute anxiety during such a reshuffling of my life circumstances. Awareness was claiming a bigger piece of the pie each and every day, and I understood how the difficult could become easy.

**What If It's Not True?**

The all too common resistance that is met with during the process of awakening is the single thought: "what if it's not true?" As a young Christian, I certainly experienced this hesitation as I approached a complex set of morals and structure which demanded my time and money, placed restrictions on with whom I could form romantic attachments or friendships, and was not bringing about happiness within me to that point. I questioned my meditation practice similarly.

As I was approaching self-realization, as the mind presented thoughts of being terrified of potential loss of its status and constructed identity, I experienced breakthroughs in which beauty and love would overwhelm my attention, and I had known this beauty and love to be my true self. These breakthroughs would be followed closely by intense fear, and the closer I was coming to this peace, the more fraught and chaotic the mind could seem at times. Fortunately, I had learned that the mind was cunning and would present such roadblocks, and so after a short time being completely derailed by this fear, I began to see it for what it was - not pertaining to anything real, simply the mind's tool to keep the status quo. In noticing this, the fear became *my* tool.

If you are finding yourself particularly subject to the mind's argument that something or someone may be lost in adopting the belief that you are the Awareness which animates all things, that this is shared among all humans, and that all other beliefs are simply aspects of the dream we are co-creating as Awareness, it will be helpful at this time to clarify and question this argument with some truly sound logic. First, this is not a belief you are adopting. You are not required to place faith in something outside of your true self, nor are you being asked to join or commit to anything. There is no money trail on the direct path, because there is no pushing of a lifelong journey of retreats and book purchases - only realization of the truth that is oneself is required to finish the journey, and this is done by seeing for oneself. The first step is the purging of all beliefs which no longer serve you - it is in doing this that you are freeing up mental space to recognize what remains - you. The second step, if we can call it that, is in doing only one thing at a time. This means when you make a sandwich, you are only making that sandwich - you are not focused on the very next moment, let alone the distant past or the uncertain future. In this moment, only this moment, in the space that is left in the absence of thought, we are inhabiting the present, and Awareness will naturally flood this space. All the content of this book ultimately amounts to the recognition that one is not the mind or beliefs, and releasing attachment to earthly constructs. There is only one truth which must be fully known and experienced, and it cannot be experienced by the mind or transmitted fully via words.

Let's say for the sake of covering all bases that I am incorrect - that the one thing which has brought boundless and causeless joy, peace, and love unlike anything previously experienced was imagined, and it was imagined after half a lifetime of meditation and searching which culminated in the genuine letting go of most of the limiting beliefs the constructed self had taken on. If it is believed that through this straightforward process which involved no spirituality whatsoever but rather an honest looking at the small self, that it was a mental breakdown, let me tell you, I highly recommend it. If one is to simply release limiting beliefs with fervor and arrive at a place of mental quiet, with no other remarkable outcomes, is this not still the most valuable hidden gem in human existence? Even if you only released three of your strongest limiting beliefs and left the rest, you would experience peace you didn't realize was possible, and it would be a challenge to leave it at just three beliefs after experiencing something like that. It is also worth noting that throughout time, many human beings who have taken the time to be alone and the trouble to differ have arrived at remarkably similar and detailed outcomes - among my favorites are Jesus, Gautama Buddha, S.N. Goenka, David Bingham, Eckhart Tolle, Krishna, Rupert Spira, Louise Hay, and several of the meditation teachers I have encountered in my years of study who have exuded the peace that is instantly recognizable by that which is peace in others. You do not need to believe me, nor do you need to believe that each of these individuals was genuinely able to demote the small self to its intended use and experience peace as their predominant state. Simply let go of any beliefs which cannot be proven, notice the subsequent lack of thoughts surrounding that particular belief, allow joy and peace to emerge, and ask yourself if you're ready to go further - to give the one Truth a proper look with an open mind free of bias, fear, and other debris. If this sounds like a lot to ask, that is because your mind is making a list of tasks to complete, as it is programmed to do. Start with one belief and one thing at a time.

### So You're Saying You're God?

It can be difficult to let go of the social constructs of shame and blame, as these have shepherded us within the bounds of what keeps us feeling safe and even loved. Many of us have the sneaking suspicion that those around us may not enjoy our rocking the boat, and for good reason - the intuition that is the real us, however ignored, is still watching, whether we know how to discern between its messages and those of the mind or not. And so, we subscribe to that which results in the least amount of external resistance - for some, that may be sports, beer, and the box. For others, that may be the right skill level in the right yoga class or belonging to the right causes.

On the whole, it is not a good look to go around calling yourself god in any way. In fact, this is a good way to get most people around you concerned for your mental health, questioning whether it's time for them to step in. My my, how things have stayed the same since the Son of God, really just trying to tell us that he was a manifestation of Consciousness and had freed himself from suffering in a series of steps he would like to share with the world, using the limited language and concepts of his time, was silenced permanently by the powers that be. The Buddha, having experienced the same liberation, found a less threatening way of communicating this and avoided making his government uncomfortable as far as I know. An important shift took place during my journey which allowed me to see things much less in black and white, and I realized that if Jesus had been a mere "normal" after all, and the Buddha had never even seemed to make claims of god status - if they were really just human avatars, then this state of liberation was truly available to all who wished it and possessed access to the will to follow through - though the ego may have been conquered, though the words may be coming from the Divine, they were still filtered through a human mind and mouth, still interpreted by the human mind, still subject to the time in which they were uttered. These words were not infallible, just as Lao Tzu said: "the Tao (Way) which can be spoken is not the true Tao." In other words, the Infinite is beyond the human mind. If the human mind and mouth can completely understand and describe it, it is not the Infinite - it is of the finite world which the mind can comprehend.

I do not profess to be The god in a way that others cannot be. I did not become something which is better than I was before, and none of this is due to merit or effort. Under the character called Heather which has existed ever since I was able to comprehend the adults around me, there is one who watches the story unfold in peaceful silence and love. That is the one true identity of all of us, and there is only one. Just as all the space in the galaxy is the same space, all the Awareness that is dreaming up this world of form is ultimately the same. There is no boundary, no distinction between the Awareness you are and the Awareness I am, to such an extent as to render this sentence and so many others nonsensical. Heather went through a great deal of struggle, so much so that the constructs she had accepted could no longer be taken as sufficient. Out of necessity, liberation was sought much like a man with his head on fire seeks water. Everything else unfolded from there. And yet, Heather is not the real me.

All spiritual teachers who are socially minded and have experienced true awakening have been through a process during their lifetimes in which suffering was transformed into fearless, causeless, boundless, timeless, and formless love and peace. The idea that the ego in individual human beings becomes upset at one teacher's message to the point that it must lash out through the individual is just a part of the game we are playing. Once one understands the process, there is no arguing with Knowing. When one has become liberated and knows how others can liberate themselves, there is often the sense that one's occupation must become the dissemination of that information, at least for a time. In this case any criticism of the method simply does not signify or register. One has fulfilled their dharma, their path, their way. If you choose to release your limiting beliefs and this leads to peace, joy, and genuine insight, it will not matter that human minds think it is arrogant to "call oneself god," a word we made up with complicated concepts seen differently from one human to the other. You've climbed the mountain, you can see all around - you can see that humans suffer needlessly, and you can see and understand the mechanisms of the mind. You are now living not as the thing but as the fabric of reality upon and within which the things exist, and you are not bothered by the entity which is threatened by this notion, because you have cleansed your inner environment from all concepts of vengeance, superiority, separateness, and anything else you had attached to it which reinforced the belief that you are small and separate. I know that at present the mindbody may be throwing up red flags, pains in the chest, headaches, or the desire to react in some big way at the reception of this argument. I know that professionals have told you to listen to your gut, that if it feels bad it is bad. While I in no way want to undermine the valid feedback the mindbody gives in situations of real danger - look deeper. Follow this experience to its source - either genuine safety mechanisms in the body or a sense that what is being said is in some way threatening to a constructed identity - and question it. Watch it change and dissolve if it is indeed rooted in a false belief. When the belief has been dismantled, ask yourself: *What if the mind is obscuring the Truth to force attention to remain on it?* Allow this openness to sit, begin to consult your inner Knowing, and watch how the world bends to reveal the Truth.

### Revisiting Forgiveness - It's For You

I have been fascinated for years at the way forgiveness has become a hot button topic, sparking heated debate amongst the wronged worldwide. I will make no attempt to sway you - I will tell my experience, having been on both sides of the argument, and I will share the insights and experiences of others. You can make your own decision.

I experienced most of my life being unwilling to forgive others unless they asked for it and demonstrated genuine remorse. This was the only way that made sense to me; why give someone something they haven't earned?

This seemed to work just fine for me until the real "wrongings" occurred. Beginning to feel that I was cursed, that those around me were incapable of understanding human emotions, that I was uniquely alone in the world - all of this accumulated over years until a sense of being unsafe was stored in my very body. You may question whether or not this is possible, in which case I will direct you to the research and life's work of Bessel van der Kolk, in particular his wildly popular book "The Body Keeps the Score." In this book, the body's ability to hang onto our past experiences as post-traumatic symptoms is laid incredibly bare from a scientific perspective. In addition, "How Healing Works" by Wayne Jonas, MD is a great scientific and observation-based read on the subject of the power of the mind to influence our health - plainly put, those who hang onto their hangups and see themselves as sick, refusing to be well, become and remain sick. Surprise, surprise. For years the mainstream has tiptoed closer and closer to an outright acknowledgement of this, and yet our society presses on, unhappy as ever, requiring things to be just so in order to be happy - ensuring our own poor health. In comes forgiveness, the key to it all.

When my symptoms reached a breaking point, when I felt so wronged that I no longer wanted to engage with society, when I expected bad things to happen and so would rather forgo the relationships, I knew that something I was doing was wrong. There were three key events in recent history which I was finding my thoughts clinging to despite the unhappiness that was felt when they landed there yet again. When I investigated very closely, I noticed that there was a part of me that got a strange kind of enjoyment from these thoughts, from my own discomfort - there was an attachment to the suffering. When I looked even closer, I noticed that when I imagined releasing this anger, that part of me said, "but then what will I think about? What will I be if not angry?" Many documented cases of coaching and therapy show that people will eventually arrive at this central realization when their lamentations are questioned. When this finally manifested as an actual thought that I could comprehend, the message was clear - a part of me was attached to suffering and didn't want it to go away. That part was extremely cunning, and had hidden itself all this time. It created roadblock after roadblock, pressured me (itself) into going out when I wanted to stay in, told me to chase friends who didn't value me - it looked for ways to perpetuate itself. I also knew that if it was a part of the small me, it could not truly wish for my demise - it was simply mistaken in its attempts, didn't have all the facts. I also saw that if it was a part of me, there were other parts - and creating agreement between these parts by investigating and dropping the beliefs I didn't really believe seemed it would take the wind out of the mind's sails to a significant degree. Then, there was the matter that if I could see that the mind was wrong... I could not be the mind.

I decided to take notice of every time I became enthralled with the very same thought process the mind had presented hundreds of times, and how these thoughts made me feel physically. When resistance to this process began to diminish, I quickly and easily noticed that I felt negative feelings in my throat, heart, and solar plexus, depending upon the type of thought it was. I found out later that these three areas are called the Triple Burner - areas of the body which are the seat of heat and tension when we experience fear. When I ruminated on having been wronged, I felt it in my heart - thanks to the awareness I had developed as a bodyworker, I could feel the pulling of the connective tissue in the body as though I was wearing a spandex bodysuit that was being cinched and pulled there, causing my chest to cave in and forward. This opened my back to vulnerability, the muscles of the spine and rear shoulder being overstretched habitually. I knew from my understanding of anatomy that when the body strays from an upright position, a significant load is added to the muscles of the neck, mid back, and low back. When this is allowed to persist, it takes great effort to open the chest and come back to the neutral position that is easy as cake for even the smallest of toddlers and all of animalkind. Emotions were pulling the body out of center, and those emotions stemmed from feelings I was holding onto about how the self had been wronged by other selves.

Whether or not you are open to the idea that we are all ultimately Divine Consciousness and pose no real threat to "each other" because there is no other and nobody is actually suffering or dying, you cannot deny that if your own feelings are pulling you out of center and this is hurting your body, and that if the emotions themselves cause you mental and emotional suffering, they are hurting you in a relative sense. So many will say, "it's okay, I've dealt with the feelings, I don't need to forgive these people." But by definition, if you are incapable of or unwilling to forgive, there is still a sense of having been wronged and needing to protect which is preventing you from being completely free of it - because believe it or not, just as Jesus covered in the Bible, when you truly forgive, you forget.

"But I don't want to forget! I don't want to give them the satisfaction, I don't want to let them back into my life, I don't want to give a shred or an inkling of an 'in' that makes them think they can repeat the behavior." You are not, not in the least. This is the center of the misunderstanding of forgiveness; we believe that to forgive is to restore full access. In fact, I am a strong advocate of forgiving and loving from a distance when one's own Knowing deems this best; it was necessary for me to create distance between myself and others very close to me, and only then did I feel safe enough to bloom, to release, and to be able to dive deeply into the work needed to release my past and beliefs. Now, having done the work, I am free to consider moment by moment whether or not this dynamic still serves me, and this is based on ongoing interaction from an objective standpoint.

During my training as a yoga teacher, a fellow student disclosed to the group that the best thing that had ever happened to her was a traumatic accident which left her with a severely impaired memory - she could no longer remember anything from before the accident, and her short-term memory was impaired. Because of this, she had lost much of what she had previously used to define herself - her story was gone. She had been able to recreate her life without long-term attachment to people, places, and things, and was able to simply gravitate toward what she liked without a lifetime of biases and habits. She was able to embrace the present moment by default much more easily than others; her expectations of herself had changed, others had different expectations of her - "she lost her memory, you can't expect her to get a job/ pursue success/ act like other people!" What a beautiful gift of freedom. This is the gift that we seek to give ourselves while retaining our general ability to remember and think - releasing ourselves from the expectations that we have bought into. We don't need to lose our memory to recognize that experiencing a human body on a planet full of chaos is not going to follow a consistent formula for everyone. This also helps us to forgive others.

Forgiveness is, after all is said and done, releasing the trapped energy in your body, the inclination toward reliving the event as though it is still a danger to you or still defines you. We can do this by simply recognizing the thoughts, feelings, and sensations when they come up, and answering these uncomfortable experiences with love and the recognition that they are not you - they won't hurt the essence of you, after all, and that essence is love. Being your true self, the Awareness that is all love and openness, in the face of these things tells the mind these situations will no longer feed it - it cannot continue to present them and expect a response. When we starve the mind of the energy it feeds on, we can watch it become entirely benign before our very eyes.

I believed I was so wronged that it would take years or even a lifetime of daily lovingkindness meditation, in which I sent everyone including my so-called oppressors love and light from a distance, to counteract and overcome the ill will and resentment that was being felt within me, finally feeling liberated at an advanced age. The belief that I was a small self called Heather was at that time still deeply entrenched. However, when I began releasing this one belief, each time the mind re-presented a scenario in which I could choose to feel offended, unsafe, or wronged, I saw how flimsy the premise was. All of this began to compound quite quickly after the first successful attempt, and in a very short time, I was detaching from the vulnerability of the small self. My true essence, and yours, cannot be harmed - when this is realized, there is nothing to fear. Living as Awareness, as one with every other being, we go a step further - there is nothing to forgive. They are you, and the sense of disconnection from this one self has understandably brought anguish. Forgiveness helps to dissolve the false boundaries.

I had spent years in fear of the increasing tension being held in my chest. My grandfather had died from a heart attack at a young age, my mother had died at a very young age from a supposed old age cancer.

I believed that because it happened to them and this body was of them, one of the two would happen to me. Eventually, I recognized that not only did I have a body with traits like theirs, I had a mind with traits learned from them - I bought their stories, their past was my past, and I was contributing my own tales of woe on top of it all. Extreme and stifled anger all around, this was the only way I knew how to operate. When I understood that the mind was but one of five interactive layers that make up the human form, I decided to change my mind and see what happened. When I dropped their beliefs, my body quit acting like their bodies. I attribute healthy blood pressure, clean colonoscopies, low-healthy liver enzymes, and otherwise unconcerning bloodwork in large part to the forgiveness I was finally able to open to, and to the relentless process of releasing that which wasn't serving me. Contrary to popular belief, this did not benefit the so-called offenders in my life one iota. However, I would be happy to see their lives transformed by this, because the part of me that was never actually harmed is the one holding the microphone.

**Resist Not**

When you resist the ease of reality, when you believe that you as a small person are in charge, in control, and responsible for using your energy to bolster and protect that small self, life will pummel you, as it did me. You will feel like a wobbly and hard ball of clay being punched against the wheel by life - no water, no centrifugal magic, no flow - just force. Your self wants you to be liberated just as much as it wants to play the game - when you are off path, you are telling the Universe exactly how to wake you up. When you decide to take on water - to soften, to go with the flow, to cooperate - then the artmaking process begins. Life is teaching you to soften, to let go of all that is false.

**The Energy Game - The Dream, Revisited**

Life is but a dream... words cleverly snuck into a children's rhyme, desensitizing and lulling us into sleep or play until we no longer hear the words as remotely real. In fact, when we hear someone say "life is but a dream," the mind goes automatically to a fanciful place, and never to the unfiltered listening of presence.

It is important that we revisit this place once more for just this reason. The entire premise of the so-called lives we are living has been made in something called mind, an extension of which has been bestowed upon humanity by Consciousness as one facet of the dream world. The thing called mind is a mechanism capable of bringing things into being - an extension of creation itself - but only when our energy is properly harnessed do we begin to intentionally create what we experience. In yoga, to become knowingly enlightened, to live in *samadhi* or continuous union with the Divine, is to drop out of the flow of karma in one's own life - no longer subject to cause and effect, to the endless cycle of birth and death, to what is called hell and was incorrectly assumed to be a place and state other than earthly and mental. Even deep in the study of yoga, I believed unity with the Divine to be something unattainable within a single lifetime and saw the Divine as other than me. The key thing that is missing from this picture: we are already it. We are Divinity itself, we are living out Divine play, we have never left a state of continuous grace. However, within this dream world, if we are not awake to that, we are still plugging our power into the dream as our sole reality - what we focus on is what permeates our experience.

Each human has its part in the experience of the dream of life as part of the collective. In "The Four Agreements," Don Miguel Ruiz refers to this as the "dream of the planet" or "society's dream." This was yet another concept which fell flat to these ears until I understood who I really am. A short time after my break from social media which played its part in awakening, I was learning to have fun again, letting go of limiting beliefs, and feeling better than I ever had, when I decided to check in with the self-compassion forum I had joined. Social media had been outside of my attention for months, the feeling of mental clearing and increased attention span had shown me that I could not go back from that, but in that moment I was seeking outside interaction within a "safe" area. I saw a post from someone asking for guidance in overcoming perfectionism. A recovering perfectionist as Heather, I offered my two cents, and found myself disappointed when the original poster reacted immediately in a way that showed she had not read my comment fully.

I decided not to engage further and told the poster they could reread my original comment - I wasn't sure if my comment had been completely free of snark or not. I found myself stewing and creating a story about this stranger - why they had asked when they didn't want an answer, how little gratitude was shown for others' time and consideration. I felt anxiety arising within, a hint of a familiar feeling of despair at humanity - then it hit me - I had co-created this situation without a doubt! After a beautiful day full of fun, insights, and inspired doing, I had logged into a public forum where anything could happen, I had engaged with a stranger while holding a set of expectations for return behavior, I had hinted at those expectations, and I had allowed a story to form which the body was now reacting to. It was all an emotional roller coaster I had buckled myself into. If I simply didn't seek keyboard interaction, my life would change. If I simply chose not to care, my life would change even more. I could stay plugged into this story and even experience sleep disturbances tonight or residue tomorrow, or I could empower myself in this moment. I could even laugh at this - the hearty laugh of one who is not affected by the dealings of humans, of one who loves all and expects nothing, yet will not tolerate mistreatment. As this one, I was safe.

There is overwhelming evidence, for those who look, that the dream we are living, when one has lost sight of their true nature, is the scenario which was described as hell. This hell, also called samsara in Sanskrit, is the continual process of birth and death in which karmic lessons must be learned by what we call souls, or extensions of Awareness. The wages of "sin," of missing the mark, is to continue to experience the chaos of earthly life without a refuge, of life in fear of "death." In this hell, the world is literally burning - humans are forced into the water to avoid the wildfire flames, our acidic food and thoughts are burning us from the inside, we have headaches, dry mouth, and colitis like never before, and most humans live in misery. More important than the circumstances is the fact that the mind churns nonstop in resistance to them, so that all doing is tinged with fear. In truth, the mental state perpetuated by the mind is the real hell. With all this suffering, do we still imagine that there is some burning, smoldering afterlife of punishment awaiting the unbelieving in this dizzying maze? Conversely, is it not sensible to see how changing our relationship to thinking, which is more chaotic than any humans before us, could have something to do with the solution to the problem? With this intensifying of chaos, of suffering, we are seeing the light rise to meet it - but only if we put ourselves in its path. Humans are awakening with unprecedented ease as they cling less and less to the dream, as the dream becomes scary enough to justify surrender even through the thickest and most stubborn mental veils. This "death for sin" transaction is a negative iteration of a reality which is incredibly uplifting when reframed - when we can transcend the game, we are ready to be done with it - to come home to who we are, which isn't even a "who." Once the mind is sufficiently open to this, it is shown to be true, and we find heaven on earth.

It may seem impossible that humanity will arrive at collective enlightenment, but this is only from the perspective of believing that each individual mind is separate from the others, and that every single human experience must be one of awakening. In fact, Consciousness can choose a new game, and can enact it through humanity. With supposed pieces of itself which can choose to enter the dream world as a human and yet are connected to and remain as the One, what helps one helps the rest - a rising tide lifts all boats, as is said. Just as a small number of animals can change the collective behavior of their group, just as adaptation occurs globally independently of contact between groups, if just a small percentage of humans are embodied knowingly by Consciousness, the collective Consciousness will shift, and the dream will shift. Additionally, when just one being becomes knowingly enlightened and lights the way for others, exponential ripples are sent out over decades and centuries. The work of the teachers called Patanjali systematized yoga, and one teacher at a well-chosen fair of world religions brought yoga to the Western masses. Now, if a revolution could take place to restore yoga to its roots - a system of purification of the small self with a light element of physical poses meant to clear debris obscuring Consciousness in the dream - which, with the internet, could be done with just one teacher or group of teachers quite quickly, the culture of yoga would change completely and become more welcoming to those of all abilities, body types, ethnicities, and belief systems than what is seen as the norm for yoga. When we take the brakes off the equipment, when we see that this is a dream, we see that one person can change the course of history entirely effortlessly, by Awareness knowingly playing that character as itself. Even better, a team of teachers acting egolessly in order to reach a ready audience can move mountains.

One of the most powerful teachings I have heard on my journey was given by David Bingham, a teacher based in England, when speaking to an individual about their sense that, although they were beginning to grasp the concepts of being one with the Divine, their mind was still running along without them, beyond their control. To this, David replied that in fact, all agency and consent has been forthcoming in this entire journey - you as what we call a soul consented to being here, and you consent to this game you are playing. In that, we are able to decide which parts of the game we wish to engage in at any given time. When we were children, we knew we were the Divine, and we had no sense of individual self - our guardians taught and reinforced the idea until we chose to take the idea on in the mind - we chose to believe it. If we hadn't been told over and over that this was the case, we would have no way of knowing it and would function as animals do, unable to understand what they are looking at in a mirror yet fully capable of protecting themselves in dangerous situations. Yes, life may have been confusing or lonely if we didn't accept this belief, but we still had a choice and we chose it. I would liken this to having realized that someone close to you was not presently capable of being a healthy companion and yet choosing to ignore it out of a desire not to be alone or on their bad side. The priorities you have taken on, which determine what you will believe, are all optional.

Perhaps even more importantly than this is the idea that before you were "packaged" into a mindbody form and found yourself on Earth as a human, you chose to go into the dream world. You chose this because you know that the real you is not harmed by anything - it is able to play in absolute bliss in a dream world that sometimes seems enveloped in pain because you are the exact opposite of that - you are not subject to pain, time, birth, death, or beliefs. You know everything. You decided to come into a family with its assets and liabilities, knowing full well that you may not retain memory of yourself, and that lack of feeling yourself would result in a human being experience that feels out of place everywhere in the dream world. That human being will not gain understanding of the Truth because it is only a character playing itself out based on Consciousness, you, in this moment; and may take on a seemingly hellish set of circumstances, but this hellishness is only because of the belief that it is you - that you are anything other than whole and complete, the Divine. Every second of every single life holds the opportunity to turn from the mind, to recognize the distinction between it and You. The second this is truly experienced, it's no wonder that fully realized mindbody after mindbody laughs and laughs, tingling with delight, upon realizing the Truth. All the suffering was based on false ideas - all of these can be dropped with ease - all the suffering has been setting us up for the most intense sense of relief, an endless appreciation for the opportunity to play in this game, this miracle of life.

When we choose to believe a narrative about this life, we plug our energy into it. The one belief that we are a separate person proliferates countless thoughts about oneself - how should I appear, what will keep me safe, how do I stop others from thinking ill of me, how do I make sure people know that I am cool... all of these thoughts abound from the one belief. When we take on another belief, perhaps that success ensures survival via social structure and that at all costs we must ensure this, our entire life is in service of that goal, and instead of seeing openly all that is before us, vision is trained on computer screens, charts, metrics, or whatever we hyperfocus on for that end. When we simultaneously believe that we must be in a happy marriage, have a family, own a home and two cars, buy cars for our children, pay for their college and weddings, maintain a reputation, take a vacation every one to two years... good luck finding time to develop any understanding of the self, whether personal or Divine. This is why so many report a feeling of finding themselves in the middle of a life they did not choose - but the unconscious part of them did choose mechanically in the game, and ultimately this is because Consciousness in this individual package has chosen to place its attention solely on the person and their interests. One individual would come to me with their troubles for years and years, always unhappy even when the perfect job was landed, the spouse got a promotion, the house with a pool was purchased, the kids were healthy. It even seemed that the more that was achieved, the more empty and frantic they felt, sensing the need to keep at a job even when they didn't like it for the sake of maintenance of all this. However, when presented with the alternative - to move to a smaller house without a pool with average schools, allowing one partner to stay home and still save money if they liked, but without the option of sending the kids to violin and karate lessons, it was unfathomable. In fact, the ego aspect created a divide between us just for my asking the question - it presented the idea that I believed myself superior, that I didn't understand, that I spoke without knowing. In fact, it was quite simple, as the Zen saying goes - "if you are not happy where you are, move - you're not a tree." Above that and considering all aspects, we have but a few choices in life, and if we simply choose one and refrain from resistance to what is, all is well. We can accept our circumstances, change them, or suffer. Yet we make it complicated. Once again, we must become unhappy enough in the circumstances we have consented to (more accurately, as a result of relative suffering we wake up to the fact that we are giving these circumstances energy with our attention) in order to finally decide to experience a different dream. All this time, we could have simply pursued the route of simplicity without having to experience turmoil first.

When we find ourselves deep in suffering, this is often when we become the most receptive to a seemingly inconvenient solution - though if it comes from another human and is directed at us personally, we are unlikely to hear above the ego's reactivity. When it comes down to it, we have two options - change the dream or change how we think about it, and either way this is achieved by disidentifying with that thinking. Imagining a third option - to fantasize about manifesting a lottery win, magically waking up without that enemy in your life, obtaining a chemical solution to a spiritual deficit, or healing the relationship without doing the work - this is a classic tactic of the mind to derail us from seeing the obvious, to create further content which gets us nowhere, to distract just a little longer. It is rooted in resistance to what already is.

"But why would I choose to insert myself into such a crazy world? Why would I knowingly be born as a person who would develop insomnia or come into this world with an inherited and incurable dis-ease? I am clearly suffering, I can't get out of that suffering - I did not consent to this!" If these thoughts are running across the mind's ticker, it is coming from a persistent identification with the mind - there is still the belief that "you" encompasses a human mind and body. There is still the belief that you live only one life, and so this one really wasn't a good one to pick. There is still the attachment to the idea that all of this *is* hurting you even on a soul level. The mind cannot grasp the deeper you, the one who has no skin in the game, who has no identification with anything in the world of form. Everything you see before you is the opposite of what you are, because you as the formless cannot be duplicated and can only create finite dream-bound forms to play with. There is still the feeling that someone else is doing this to you, because even if you do not subscribe to a religion, your mind is still subject to influence from a prevailing societal idea that we are helpless and created by a separate being, and that we are not good enough, and these ideas tend to seep into the collective through story. You as Awareness are strong enough - you as Awareness are not affected by time. In your realm, you are dreaming a dream which is taking no time at all to unfold, just as the night dreams of humans do not subscribe to the typical constraints of time that daydreams and all other thoughts seem to.

When we realize that we have been plugging energy into various amusements that mind labels "good" and "bad," that we have chosen to be on the ride of emotions or to be completely enveloped by the mind by adopting beliefs which perpetuate these states, the choice is obvious - get off the ride. Let the thoughts race by, stop feeding them, see the entire dream and not just the corner in which you've been banging your head. Take off the bifocals, definitely toss that fish eye lens in the trash, and see the whole picture. To realize that one has been afraid of the uncertainty and vulnerability of not knowing how life will unfold, that the mind's churnings are there in some effort to create an internal world in which we can affect the tone and filter of the dream, in which control is seemingly restored - in realizing this, all becomes easy. Drop control, unplug your energy from all stories and all effort. Notice that the mind's thoughts are about 95% repetitive, pointless, and false - and realize you cannot possibly be that if you can realize that about them. In this moment, consent to a different reality - you will now live the reality where the mind is your tool, only used when needed. With the mind at rest, 95% of the energy consumed by mental fluctuations becomes yours again - think what you could do with that! It is from this place that we can begin to live from the intuition and inspiration which will naturally and quickly flood any space that is made for them - the doing of the human is experienced effortlessly and joyfully, and entirely unto itself, with no requirements of outcome placed on it whatsoever. This is surrender.

# CHAPTER EIGHT

## KNOWING AND DOING WHAT YOU WANT

When we say the mantra or prayer "Thy will be done," what is it we are saying? We are telling the Universe that the individual package of Consciousness surrenders any sense of its own will as a person, that it is decided that Divinity is the source of all wisdom, that for life to go well the personal will must be aside and allow that all is done for the highest good of the essential self that is living every life. So - how do we do that?

Many of us possess zero insight into how we would go about living solely through inspiration and intuition - we've been trained to follow the fold, to go straight from high school to work or more school, to act in accordance with each entity's culture to avoid being removed, and to juggle the many other priorities of humans like social obligation, religious or philosophical practice, and somehow to manage our financial affairs and raise a family, often without the support of the community requiring so much from us. Many realize only too late that they actually never wanted a job in the traditional sense, never wanted to trade time for money, never wanted to be bound to one place for eighteen years while children grow up to emulate those around them, or actually rather prefer their own company and that of friends and family to a partner. By the time we realize it, we feel trapped, and so we live our lives in Thoreau's quiet desperation. Run naked into a lake? *Someone will see! I will be arrested! It's wrong!* Frolick in a meadow? *Where does one even find a meadow in these parts! Who has the time!* Start a business? *But I have it on good authority that I'm dumb and don't follow through on things! But I didn't go to business school!*

*But my family doesn't seem excited when I talk about it, so my idea must not be good and wouldn't appeal to others!* When you see just how tightly wound minds are around the societal rulebook, that an entity has been created within the mind just to judge and keep itself within the confines of society... the first thing you may want to do is throw away all your clothes and join a nudist community in close proximity to both a lake and a meadow. I'll let inspiration and intuition tell you whether that's the right long-term call for you.

Once you get the repressed energy out of your system and your system trusts that you will honor it, you will find that your desires come about in a much calmer and more decided way. *I have two hours of free time, I want to go to the park and lay on a blanket.* No feelings of *if I go to the park I might run into someone I know and that will take up the energy I need to run my 4:00 meeting.* First of all, meetings and all other things you choose to do will become effortless when you no longer expend internal energy on the thoughts preserving that identity you made. Second, you will no longer be plugging your energy into society's outlet, so your energy will be yours to give as you choose - all will be a matter of realizing and executing. Conversations will require little to no energy when there is no sub-program commentating on the whole thing and trying to keep the person within the bounds of proper speech when you approach them from love rather than fear. When you want a snack, you get one. When the body presents excessive churnings for snacks, you heed the wisdom to recognize that more than a snack, you want a healthy mindbody. Over time, these spontaneous ideas will manage themselves, always in line with the needs of the bodymind. In this, there is no suppression of desire - only a weighing and harmonizing.

**I Am The Glue...**

There is a sense within many humans, a dread of sorts, that if they did what they wanted, society would collapse. If jobs are so terrible and everyone decided not to have them, there would be no means of commerce, of attaining the things that have kept us occupied. Of course, this is missing the fact that if we were happier the collective dream would no longer require constant generation of new ways to occupy one's mind. There will be droves of people who say that these things make us happy or stem the suffering of this world or that we deserve them, but this choice to carry on with someone else's dream comes from fear and ignorance of the unknown, a side effect of the mind's habitual patterns of protection and the supposed vulnerability of straying from those. We might look at the world around us and say, "everyone's eyes look empty, nobody will talk about what's really going on, I wish I had better people around me," and then in our unhappiness pop to the shop for snacks made of sugar designed to take us on a roller coaster that feels a bit like being truly alive; so occupied by our thoughts of doom that we make eye contact with none of the people we see along the way. It's like we're saying, "society is bad but we're all too tired and addicted to the side effects, let's just feed into it."

The system itself is quite flimsy, held together only by our collective misunderstanding that humans are the only species unbalanced enough to require constant governance from all sides. All this stems from the misunderstanding that we *are* humans, and not the Divinity peeking out from the machines most capable of either knowingly embracing reality or using outsized powers to distort it. Fortunately, many are waking up to the fact that the system is not exactly designed intelligently. We can now relate more than ever to the limitations of artificial intelligence, and when we consider minds to be the original artificial intelligence, and excessive attention placed on mind is basically creating a system designed without the real thing, this hits deeply. A bunch of individuals with conflicting desires are a sad replacement for a cohesive unit of minds as tools, without opinions of their own (yes, I just said that), working in tandem. The entire system is exactly the way it is because of the collective input into it; most people believe they were happier before smart phones existed, and yet nobody wants to be the first one to chuck theirs in the nearest phone recycling kiosk - we now "need them to survive, to get along within the system." I have experimented in different ways with this - with leaving my phone at home and noticing the sense that I am in danger without it; with downgrading my device to a prepaid non-smart phone; with designating Sundays as entirely screen-free days. Always, there is the sense that something might happen to a loved one during those minutes or hours, or something will develop on the internet which finally brings people truly closer together, and I'll miss it. Forget the fact that in my entire life, this has never happened. What's more, as the owner of a bodywork business, I told myself that I could not thrive without a solid online presence, would upset people when texts weren't responded to on Sundays, would miss something important. That subscription to the system eventually told me exactly the beliefs which needed to be overcome - exactly where my fears and attachments were.

Several years ago, someone very close to me had just returned from a year abroad and had fallen into a depression at seeing the state of things in the U.S. She lamented not being able to stop at any corner bakery for her pesticide-free daily bread; she missed speaking the language; she missed a culture where it felt safe to just be average, running a moderate small business or working the same job until one retired; she missed the mood, the parties, the scenery. What's more, because of the intensity of this feeling and the subsequent thoughts which captivated her for years, she took little pleasure in what her present surroundings had offered her, keeping to her dark apartment and feeling too exhausted after work to do much of anything.

Though she desperately wanted to return to the country she loved, she determined that it was nearly impossible. In her intellect-driven experience, only if she attained a very specific kind of job could she envision being able to make it back; but then, education was so expensive. She decided to get married and have children, resulting in circumstances seeming to tie her to her job. Even when she worked for a company that would pay for her education, she did not attend the classes needed for that specific kind of job; circumstances now prevented it.

I found myself living in Hawai'i at age twenty, in a bungalow a mile from the ocean and just outside a lovely little town in which I enjoyed regular walks. One day, my husband at the time told me he was being let go for failing to meet his military requirements multiple times; the dire nature of which I had not been made aware. Suddenly, there was a choice - head back home now with all expenses paid for, or stay in Hawai'i indefinitely, hoping the same husband would quickly get a job and retain it in order to help me pay our significant rent bill. I decided to go back "home," but I too lamented my lost life circumstances, and shortly after developed severe anxiety. I have had consistent dreams for almost two decades of that place.

In both of these stories, there were choices - ensure some kind of stability within a societal structure, or simply do what one wants to do with faith that all will be well. When you muddy the waters and assume things like "I will surely struggle financially here," "financial struggle will make me so unhappy," and "the ease of having an affordable house payment will outweigh the loss of this thing which I love and appreciate," you are valuing society's dream over yours.

Instead, if the initial pangs of anxiety were sensed upon thinking about being without a strong safety net, and those pangs were understood to be reminders that we had lost sight of our own way, we could work through the thing that is astray with us instead of carrying on with a life devoid of authenticity. When we learn to recognize these initial signs, to bring them under the light and scrutiny of Awareness, and to release any limiting beliefs that are resulting in this anxiety, the path is clear.

I heard an extremely powerful spoken word clip years ago that has stayed with me. In it, the speaker walks through a hypothetical dialogue that goes something like this: *"why do you think we're here?* To be happy. *What do you want out of life?* To be happy. *Well, how do you do that?* I do things that make me happy. *Yes, but to what end?* I'm happy doing them, and then they make me happy." This was yet another encounter with simple clarity which I mistook for overly simplistic, missing the profundity of the words in the first listen; it was the speaker's confidence which caught me, so I listened again. Suddenly, it hit me - just as the Buddha said, when this is the entire point of our being here, it's quite simple. Happiness is both the means and the end. Stay in Hawai'i if you like it. Stay in the same house your whole life if it truly makes you happy. Bring your kids on an RV ride across the country if it brings out full-fledged joy, and they will have a model for happiness and free being for the rest of their lives. Sell the big house and get the small house if it allows you to realize your dream of early retirement and travel. Get the big house if you really want it, and if it turns out not to be the end all, get rid of it - just as long as you don't lament a loss of investment or of others' supposed respect. The key here is non-attachment, not the actual circumstances - considering this lifetime as an experiment among many, and while appreciating your time here, not seeing it as something you must stretch thin in your one and only go-round. Do all things with the ease and clarity of already being happy, and from this vantage point, easily able to see that which you as happiness attract to you. It was in finally releasing the belief that one must exercise, cook a healthy dinner, make an effort to go out and do new things, and have a life others envy in order to be living fully that finally allowed me the opportunity to quit an unhealthy job, decide not to get another one right away, buy the small house, completely ignore what was happening on television, social media, and even the news so that I could sit long enough in clarity and ease, spend enough time in the pursuit of understanding the true self to allow the lessons to permeate past a mere intellectual understanding, feeling happiness at the cellular level and beyond. It is and has always been that simple.

**How Will I Know?**

So, you've let go of the idea that society needs you to fit into it in order to fully function. You've dropped some of the things you were doing which were clouding the view, occupying your time, and demanding your resources, freeing up space. How do you know if the next thing is something you really want to do or something the mind is still attached to? First of all, you do not need to have this all figured out in one go (read that again) - the idea that you do is a human construct, the very programming you are looking to disidentify with. Yes, this may mess with your mind for a while; that's okay. The way you will know something comes from a pure and authentic inner desire is the way you will feel about it - there will be no pressure to attain it, no need to force it, no need to convince anyone to let you have it.

A side effect of living as the true self is a complete lack of effort, and when we release the belief that life must be forced, it shows us quickly that the contrary was always true - we were in our own way. When life becomes easy, what you want will present itself to you, will accept you, will love you, will be compatible with all that serves your highest good. This requires some faith - after what might seem like a lifetime of failure, and with no evidence to the contrary, you are supposed to believe that you are infinite and failure is just an illusion? There will be no evidence except those humans you encounter who claim to have lived otherwise, and perhaps a deep inner resonance despite the mind's resistance when you hear things like "you are the love you seek." Whether you feel this deeply or become engrossed in the mind's surface-level production of the play that says "all new age books are out of touch," you have exactly the message you need in order to know what to do next. Either enjoy the resonance and begin to test your new understanding, or notice the messenger - the red flag telling you your reaction to this thing is making you feel bad - notice the belief behind it, question whether or not you've ever been able to verify it as universally true, and when you inevitably answer "no," release the belief. After releasing the belief, notice what remains.

### Inspired and Intuitive

Imagine if everything you did, all day, every day, was inspired and intuitive. You might imagine this to look something like being on vacation - wake up, make brunch, sit on the beach, make dinner, do the dishes, go for a hike, sit on the beach. Some might say, *if all I did all day was what I want, nothing would ever get done!* This is because those people are overworked and depleted - they are likely not doing work that gives them any joy, and may equate work with suffering. For years I dreamt of nothing but early retirement; my experience of corporate life was that it had seemed to conflict with spiritual growth. Later I ran my business, made connections, and did worthwhile work which encouraged my growth, but I couldn't get over the deeply engrained idea forged during corporate drudgery - I wanted to be out of the race as soon as possible. I would occasionally ask myself, *If I were done working tomorrow, what would I do with my time?* While I'd want a little rest time, I knew the inspiration to have a purpose goes deep and tends to occur naturally when not repressed. I considered this question for some time until I realized something very important - *I don't want to retire early; I want to be able to retire early! Even deeper than this; I simply want to be free of financial constraint so my work can be inspired, and I can give this to myself right now!* My true desire could not have been clearer: I want to be happy. And without interference of mind, I can be happy without changing anything.

Once you spend a little time in self-inquiry asking yourself the tough questions, it becomes quite easy to see how you would like to spend your time without the constraints of societal pressure or supposed requirements. You will feel an urge arise, but within that urge is a happiness that is not dependent upon the having or doing of that thing. You are happy, so you do that thing, and that thing makes you happy. This may run counter to all the programming centered around "deserving a break," "earning respect," or "striving for peace," but you neither need to earn nor work toward happiness. You need to stop struggling against it, stop making it conditional via your belief system.

Living life as an extension of Divine play means that you don't need to quit anything you're doing. You can if you want - but if you don't, you will approach it differently. You watch the doing happen with joy. The difference is the energy you bring to it - when you are acting as Awareness, all is play.

## Does My Happiness Make Me Look Selfish?

One way that our belief systems prevent us from being happy is by attaching fulfillment to selfishness. Many hold the hidden or outright belief that those who do not wish to have children are selfish - that belief is beginning to crumble in the face of climate change, and is now seen by some as a compassionate sacrifice. Talk about a belief built on sand! Some believe parents should sacrifice their evenings in favor of taxi duty; others describe the practice as creating entitled and even codependent adults. Many believe that those who do not make themselves unhappy over what they see in the news are selfish, while those who experience peace without it know that it makes them much more capable of doing what needs done for the things they care about.

The point is, nobody agrees on all facets of an existence rooted in a morality constructed by the fickle mind. Our minds are thus because attention is placed on the individual as the center of their world - intelligent co-creation is a built-in feature of this dream world which is being suppressed. This is why young children are so upset at having will suppressed - they may not be able to verbalize it, but they know their Divine right, and they are experiencing feeling thwarted. Once one returns to this understanding, they may never look at the Terrible Twos in the same way.

Shortly after I quit my job and found myself neck deep in creativity and freedom, I was presented with another job opportunity. I went in for an interview knowing that I did not care whether I got this job or not - I was thousands of words away from publishing a book which would help those with whom it resonated, and I was experiencing a wonderful new confidence, a Knowing, that this was what I wanted to be doing. This is, in fact, a misnomer, an example of the shortcomings of our words and concepts; that Knowing was me, and I was living as it. The outcome didn't matter; publishing, popularity, and all other factors were secondary to these: *am I inspired? Is intuition flowing? Am I enjoying it?* Without a doubt. This is how we do what we want - from a place of wholeness, worthiness, and ease. What's more, surrender had occurred - I no longer wanted a job that didn't want me, so if it didn't work out, I was happy to leave it behind. Shortly after that, I began applying this to the new relationships I was forging. The result was a life that was a direct reflection of the wholeness being revealed; each "no" to what no longer served me became a "yes" to that which I truly was, and the more I showed myself, the more the world came to me.

The teacher Rupert Spira says in one of his talks that to approach spiritual growth always from a place of obligation, as in required and excruciating daily seated meditation or dietary sacrifice which leaves you feeling shorted, is disrespectful to the process. I had thousands of hours of demoralizing efforts toward mindfulness under my belt when I first heard the lecture containing that sentiment, so the intensity of the word "disrespectful" stung for a moment, but only a moment. It was wonderfully clarifying - my pattern of dogmatic religious worship had been carried forward into spiritual seeking, looking for the Big Boss outside of me to add their thoughts to the Big Boss inside of me to tell me what to do, how to think and act. This could be easy instead. It was with this realization that my meditation practice immediately discontinued, causing no guilt whatsoever. I didn't want to do it, and I enjoyed a great many other things involving determination and dedication. I had long suspected that I might be experiencing that tendency which a doctor would deem "ADHD," which I saw as a naturally adapted strong tendency to avoid the present rather than a disorder, and had long attempted to box in the mental energy I had access to - just for a while, I was going to let it loose. If it all fell apart without my practice, I'd simply bring it back with an increased appreciation. But nothing fell apart except my belief that a continuous and traditional sitting meditation practice was necessary. The habitual dread faded, and in surged the creative energy which resulted in way after way that I could use that time and energy. Walking meditation in nature, kite flying, mindful house cleaning, daily watercolor practice, and gardening all seemed like preferable ways to focus the mind on only one thing at a time, inhabiting the present moment. As I realized this, it occurred to me that the many humans who opt out of meditation for lack of available time or a guilt at doing nothing could much more easily adopt a practice of this kind - one rooted in compassion for those living in a society that collectively demands too much. This was love for the self, the very balm we need.

### Discernment: The Key to Happy Doing

During my training to become a yoga teacher, the word "discernment" was presented many times as a key to greater understanding. Though ultimately we endeavor to go beyond the mind as a master, while it continues to carry on nonstop we can learn to tell the difference between truth and fiction. This can be quite subtle, and ultimately comes down to accurate understanding of our thoughts and feelings. Revenge might feel "good" for a moment, but carries with it a deep tension requiring our focused attention to detect, and typically does not allow us to release our anger or experience lasting happiness. The act itself also does not bring anything good to us - we "sin" against ourselves by creating further discord with one whose life is being lived by the same entity that we ultimately are. So, before you do anything, knowing whether your choice is ecological, whether it will be done from joy, and whether it is necessary are all things to consider. Just because the mind prefers many things does not mean they all need done in a day, or that each day needs to be filled with them. Just because the mind presents ideas of travel, an idea that humans lived without for most of our time on earth, does not mean that you have to in order to be happy. Just because you don't presently have the bank balance for daily shop coffee or regular pedicures, also things past generations didn't consider to be normal or even possible, doesn't mean you are missing out on anything really necessary, if we stay to the true purpose of existing as a human, which is not the attainment of pleasurable experiences but the recognition of one's true nature. Enlightened doing is a beautiful convergence of the small self and the higher self - Awareness wants to do it, Awareness has lined up the circumstances, and the mindbody called Heather is capable of being the vehicle needed to do it, so it's easy, natural, and joyful.

### Spiritual Journeying - A Distraction from What Is

Growing up in church, I was taught to release all ideas of attaining wealth - strangely enough, among a congregation of the comparatively wealthy. I understood this to mean that wealth was inherently bad. As an adult, my guilt over the acquisition of any good fortune meant that I questioned myself any time I had to "market" my value in a job.

When I encountered Buddhism, I zeroed in on the Four Noble Truths - in life there is suffering, the cause of this suffering is attachment to things going a specific way, there is a way from suffering, and that way is through the Eightfold Path - purifying the self in eight all-encompassing areas of life.

To my understanding at the time and indeed the way it is sometimes conveyed, my repressed little self took these truths to mean that desire of any kind is bad. In fact, it is not desire that leads to suffering but the attachment to desire from the perspective of the person - the belief that life should go a certain way for me. When we attach to good things and push bad things away, we have "eaten of the fruit of the tree of good and evil" - the mind has become programmed to be polarized, to buy into the concept that this is good and that is bad; we have placed conditions upon our being happy, which is counter to our nature as loving and stable Awareness. There is no Divine punishment - there is simply the cause - conditional happiness - and the effect - a lack of happiness, which would otherwise flow freely.

Using the discernment we are learning to cultivate, we allow desire to come up within us - it's only natural. We may act on that desire or not - what is important is that we do not become attached to a specific outcome. When my extreme attachment to the body and subsequent fear of being injured was worked through, I suddenly experienced a strong desire to try much more daring types of new experiences like kayaking in a cavern and learning the art of firewalking. Subsequently, I met the people who enjoyed these activities, widening my circle to include those who were similarly less fearful of loss of the body, and this quickly affected the way my nervous system felt and the tendencies I was picking up from my environment. With one shift, it became much easier to reinforce my new understanding. Additionally, I learned where I had gone astray within a spiritual practice, and even began to see it differently - not as spiritual, but as quite a practical way to release the experience of suffering. After all, "spiritual" was just a label created by humans to describe the process for those who were not currently experiencing continuous union with the Divine - when in continuous understanding that we are Divinity itself, we know that such a label for a specific experience isn't necessary. In other words, what we think is mystical is simply that for which we do not yet have an explanation.

As my journey found lightness, as I began to associate less and less with labels and concepts, it became clear to me that morality was something invented by humans. My favorite teachers all echoed the same sentiment - that we are here to be happy, to do what we want, and only when that is suppressed do our desires become imbalanced or out of alignment with our higher self. The very fear that humans left to their own will make the wrong choices is why humanity is now the only species requiring the need for governance, law enforcement, and mental health support - our beliefs and subsequent actions perpetuate such a reality. To differ from such a system takes great courage at times, but your very life is gained.

# CHAPTER NINE

## EXERCISES

Until now, we've just been looking at Consciousness from a distance, perhaps coming a little closer with each new way of phrasing and understanding with the intellect. There may be imaginary roadblocks remaining on our path to clear seeing. Next, we go into greater detail and look at practical ways we can begin to shift our view of the world bit by bit.

There are many exercises we can do with regularity to bring us closer to realizing the Awareness that we are, embodying the present moment and doing only one thing at a time - that is, embodying Awareness, letting doing flow without interference of mind. Eventually, this one thing at a time will end up feeling more like being that doing - doing is happening, while here I am being, observing. While we are looking at a variety of practices over a broad range of disciplines, it bears repeating that the most important part of all of this is to release limiting beliefs, to learn to weather the fluctuations of the mind without reaction, and to come to realize that we are not the mind or the body - that there is space between the "I" and the "me." All the yoga in the world is not going to bring you to that realization unless you keep your intention, *sankalpa* in Sanskrit, close to you. We are not here to get distracted in the game of life, though we can certainly lean into it fully - we are taking part in it while realizing that we are not of this world, merely visiting.

Several exercises will just touch the tip of the iceberg of the traditions they represent. Some exercises may not be necessary if you already employ similar practices - for instance, if you are already a dancer, rock climber, painter, or participant in anything that brings you into a flow state, that state in which the chatter of the mind subsides either through joy or from the "controlled danger" bringing about a naturally heightened state of presence, you might find awareness practices fun but unnecessary. It is important here to distinguish from heightened states of consciousness and the realization of one's true nature. Heightened states may or may not bring about self-realization indirectly depending upon the person, while self-realization is simply a knowing, not an experience, but can result in heightened states naturally. Ultimately, none of these exercises will lead you to the realization of the true self if you simply choose to run through them daily, adding content to the ego and deriving some sort of pride from any newfound abilities. These are stepping stones to be left behind as soon as you see fit - ultimately, you consult your inner Knowing as to whether something is for you. All is to be done from inspiration, intuition, and joy. If not, either find the joy in it or simply don't do it. Yes this flies in the face of a duty-bound societal code, no it is not selfish in any negative sense, yes this attitude is precisely how you begin to embrace the free and autonomous being that you are.

Some basic videos illustrating some of these exercises are available on my website. There are plenty more available online, or other methods of learning more if these exercises resonate with you. With this in mind, may these exercises bring you closer to realizing the peace that you already are.

## Beliefs - Inventory, Analysis, and a Daily Cliff Drop

Some teachers of self-realization reached the state we call enlightenment simply through the releasing of limiting beliefs. Spoiler: when you have successfully released a few beliefs and experienced the spaciousness and relief that immediately follow, you will quickly realize that all beliefs are limiting - when we commit to this level of release, we are accessing Divine will and intuition, which will lead to our seeing all that has been going on beyond our view of the mind's chatter. When people report experiencing an epiphany, suddenly seeing colors more vividly, and experiencing their food with more gratitude, this is the Awareness that they already are, the capacity to be happy and grateful for every part of this journey, sitting just behind the mind waiting for us to realize it. And while these experiences can be pleasing and interesting, they are not required in order for us to realize the truth of what we are.

It can be helpful at first to take an active approach to recognizing beliefs by spending some time writing them down and answering questions about them. This exercise has been modified from Byron Katie's practice called "The Work", Louise Hay's exercise in recognizing the origins of our beliefs, and the techniques learned in training as a coach. These exercises were instrumental in allowing transcendence of the mind's programming and understanding what I truly am - however, I found that as I practiced, I had my own way of approaching it. I am grateful to these teachers for their foundational work.

Find a quiet place and begin to think about the beliefs that you hold about yourself and life. Also consider any beliefs you think others hold about you that you have bought into on some level. Maybe you believe yourself smarter than most, maybe you feel that others think you are lazy. Write down the belief, where it came from, and how this belief makes you feel, using the messengers we introduced in Chapter 2: limited, time-bound, lacking, confused/disconnected, and incomplete.

*Example 1: Others believe I don't follow through on things. This comes from the fact that I am often taking up new hobbies or jobs and dropping old ones. When I believe this, I feel limited, lacking, disconnected, and incomplete.*

*Example 2: I believe I am ugly. This comes from my parent's regular criticism and unhealthy societal norms. When I believe this, I feel limited, lacking, and incomplete.*

Get as detailed as you like - this inventory, right in front of you, is the work you will be doing to realize the joy directly behind your beliefs. This, right here.

Now, look at each belief and ask: *is it universally true? Can I prove it?* A big hint: nothing that is subjective is universally true, and even much that we find objective that is based on our limited sense organs should be seen as just that - not one single limiting belief is going to hold up to scrutiny, otherwise it would be called a fact and not a belief.

When you inevitably realize, one after another, that each belief you have held about yourself and the world is false or open to interpretation, your worldview becomes rather shaky - if you only believe in that which can be proven through direct experience and is not subject to sensory organs which only pick up 1% of what is really going on around us, you won't believe much at all - and that is the freedom you seek. In fact, to "believe in" your direct experience without interference of mind is to Know, and is beyond doubt because all variables and faulty equipment have been removed from the equation. All of the thoughts associated with all of these beliefs will begin to weaken and dissipate, and suddenly, there won't be much to think about. The utter simplicity and effectiveness of this one exercise alone is enough to make you cry tears of joy when you get the hang of it. Once it becomes habit, you will notice thoughts and beliefs in real time and automatically correct them effortlessly - the joy you feel in doing this cannot be compared to anything you've felt until now.

Bonus: When beliefs are feeling quite heavy, which may for many be every day, an excellent practice to adopt is to imagine yourself carrying a stack of books, each book holding the title of one of your beliefs, maybe in your arms or perhaps in a backpack, up a tall winding staircase leading to the stars. Feel the heaviness, notice drops of sweat forming from carrying the weight. When you reach the top, you find a platform with a railing. Take your stack of books and drop them over the side, watching them plummet under the spell of gravity, feeling yourself becoming lighter and lighter with each book as you watch them fall to the earth, or perhaps become weightless and float into the stars.

**So What?**

It can take some time to cultivate your understanding of the subtler and lesser known thoughts and beliefs, and further time still to really see how false every single belief really is. Once you have an understanding of these beliefs and have begun developing a willingness to see yourself and life without them, you can add to it the following practice. The first time you successfully execute this, you will feel on top of the world - able to see a glimpse of how Awareness, love, can conquer every thought that has ever weighed on you.

I first learned this practice in a slightly varied form through Cognitive Behavioral Therapy about ten years ago. Even back then I valued eventually becoming one's own therapist, so I took a 12-week course which was meant to give one all the tools they need to talk back to the mind. During one session, as complaining streamed and coursed from the mind, my therapist simply asked, "so what?" I was taken aback, and my mind stopped. Suddenly, I saw - if I only answered the constant objections of the mind with this one question, their power was lost. I've since come to understand that this practice can reset the body - it is instrumental in divesting attention from thought and emotion, which diminishes the effects they have.

I learned another, deeper version of this practice in reading "The Greatest Secret" by Rhonda Byrne, the book that redirected my attention into nonduality and to realization of the self. In this book, Rhonda describes a practice she learned from various teachers, sometimes called Welcoming, in which we answer the resistance of the mind with non-resistance. Though the mind really didn't like the idea of "welcoming" negative thoughts, there was willingness to consider the idea of letting go of resistance. So, until I could find the courage to welcome and actually open the energetic and physical heart space to the pain the mind was distracting from, I simply practiced letting go - letting it be there. It wasn't quite welcome, but I wasn't trying to stop it.

I realized later in my practice that this was the very same mechanism that I had unsuccessfully attempted in my journey with Vipassana meditation. *Vipassana* is the Sanskrit word for "seeing things as they really are," and I was incredibly frustrated during my efforts with this (effort being my first mistake) to find that I had seemingly zero ability to accept reality as it is. I know now that a great deal of my resistance came from feeling stuck in a silent retreat for ten straight days, and had I been able to digest the material on my own time and in my own place, I may have taken it in with a completely different tone and intention. Realizing that this was the same thing as welcoming, and as "so what," I was free to enjoy the process.

When a feeling comes up in the mind, or if you experience an uncomfortable sensation in the body, to welcome or allow the feeling to exist just as it is, without trying to change it, is the practice of a lifetime. Not because it takes a lifetime to achieve, but because in practicing it you gain a lifetime of happiness.

As you recognize a negative feeling or sensation, bring your attention to it for only a moment, and soften to the experience - widen your attention to take in the entire experience, literally softening body and mind, as you find a sense of total safety in what has been seen as an unsafe experience. I like to laugh good-naturedly at the machinations of the mind, seeing how little and insubstantial they are, like watching a child become upset. They think the world is crumbling, and all is well. The freedom in being the knower of that is the vantage point we are looking for. We create a layer of separation between the "I" and the "me" - and the "me" can't touch the "I." It's funny!

Over time, the mind loses power. In fact, it only ever had all that power because you believed you were it, and that belief placed your creative energy into the mind, making it so. This exercise reinforces the dropping of your inventory of beliefs and creates space between you and what you experience. The more space you create, the less real the false becomes.

**Body Awareness**

Though our ultimate goal is to release the beliefs which hold us back from seeing reality as it is, we acknowledge that the mind and physical body are layers to the human experience as a whole, interacting with one another intimately. When we experience a dysregulated nervous system, it can be difficult to find the sense of safety required to really take in new ideas. So, making friends with the physical body is an excellent way to make friends with the mind and allow that space to open.

*Progressive Muscle Relaxation*

This method is offered by yoga teachers, therapists, and spiritual teachers of all kinds. It is easy to follow, easy to pick up, and incredibly relaxing. This practice can also release blockages in the body placed there by stuck emotions.

Start by sitting or lying in a comfortable position, and systematically, the same way each time, work through the different parts of the body, tensing, holding, and releasing. Tense and hold for five seconds, noticing the quality of the tension; then release, and hold for ten seconds while you notice how it feels for that muscle to be completely relaxed. So often we tense without realizing it, and this practice helps us to gain awareness and control over our muscles, as well as gaining control over our response to sensations. A few different scripts are offered in the companion to this book.

A sample script:

*Begin by finding a comfortable position either sitting or lying down in a location where you will not be interrupted.*

*Allow your attention to focus only on the body. If you notice the mind wandering, bring it back to the body.*

*Take a deep breath into the belly, allowing it to rise. When the belly is full, continue to breathe into the chest. Allow the breath to leave the belly, then the chest, effortlessly. Continue this breath through the exercise.*

*Tense the eyebrows inward toward each other. Hold for 5 seconds. Release and hold for 10 seconds. Notice the breath, and notice the difference in sensation.*

*Tense the forehead by raising the eyebrows. Hold for 5 seconds. Release and hold for 10 seconds.*

*Open the jaw and mouth wide. Hold for 5 seconds. Release and hold for 10 seconds.*

*Tense the back of the neck gently. Hold for 5 seconds. Release and hold for 10 seconds. Continue to notice the change in sensation, in effort, from tense to relaxed.*

*Tuck the chin, lengthening the back of the neck. Hold for 5 seconds. Release and hold for 10 seconds.*

*Make fists and contract the arms in, as making a muscle. Tense the entire arm. Hold for 5 seconds. Release and hold for 10 seconds.*

*Bring the shoulder blades together. Hold for 5 seconds. Release and hold for 10 seconds.*

*Tense the abdomen. Hold for 5 seconds. Release and hold for 10 seconds.*

*Point the toes, tensing the underside of the feet, the calves, and continue through the hamstrings to the glutes. Hold for 5 seconds. Release and hold for 10 seconds.*

*Contract the toes up toward the knees, tensing the shins and the quadriceps muscles. Hold for 5 seconds. Release and hold for 10 seconds.*

*Now tense every muscle in the body. Hold for 5 seconds. Release and hold for 10 seconds.*

*Notice the change in sensation from tensed to relaxed. Recognize the effort in tensing, the effortlessness in releasing, and the effortless registering of the difference in sensation. Notice that there is effort, and there is your effortless awareness of sensation.*

*Continue to breathe deeply for a few more breaths, allowing all muscles to deepen into this relaxation.*

There are different variations on scripts you can use, and a sample video available on my website, or you can combine them and use wording that feels best to you. Once you're comfortable with the practice, recite your script into a voice recorder so that you learn to take direction from yourself. Eventually, when you tell your body to relax, it will listen, no matter what is going on around you.

*Yoga Nidra*
Yoga nidra is similar to PMR, but with a twist - it combines elements of our "So What" activity by shifting the attention from one body part to another in swift succession, encouraging the mind to notice without ruminating or judging. This is a form of retraining the mind to recede, allowing for observation without judgment. This has also been called "yogic sleep," and certain forms of yoga nidra are designed to overcome Post-Traumatic Stress Disorder and insomnia. From the depths of excessive mind-based suffering, we return to the ease and simplicity of effortless noticing. Examples of this practice abound, so find the variation that suits you. Scripts and videos are offered on my website.

**One Thing At A Time**
This exercise is so simple, yet at the heart of this book and the journey. It took years for my mind to recede enough that I understood and took this fundamental process seriously. If you find that your mind says "what's the big deal, I feel no different," bring to awareness the distinction between the voice and you. And do it again. And again.

Thich Nhat Han wrote his books "Peace is Every Step" and "Peace is Every Breath" based on one simple principle, the same one that has echoed through this book and ultimately what Zen Buddhism and even religion is all about. To do only one thing at a time - to embody the one simple task that you are doing, to give all troubles to the governing force of the Universe that you ultimately are so that you can experience this, here, and now, is the powerful way that we relax back into our true nature. To do this while also knowing that you are the stillness that is always present beneath thoughts and actions will only amplify your practice.

This is a very practical way to introduce mindfulness into your life if you haven't already, because it requires nothing from you. You do not need to cut out any activities or neglect your kids, partner, or friends in order to practice this. It begins to work from where you already are and with what you are already doing.

Begin to designate several activities each day that you already complete, which you will now begin to practice in mindfulness. Mindfulness is to incorporate awareness and acceptance into the present moment - to notice all that arises in this field of relaxed open attention, and to allow all, ultimately one, to be exactly as they are. It is helpful at this stage not to think of this as meditation, because with that comes baggage - bias, set ideas about how that looks, and a certain kind of effort or outcome that might become more likely. Let go of the outcome, and simply do this one thing with the clean curiosity of a child.

There are many activities which lend themselves well to this practice: laundry, dishes, walking the dog, feeding the cat, eating, taking the stairs or elevator to the office, walking from the office to the parking garage. All of these activities are usually completely consumed in pointless and repetitive thought - you are simply reclaiming this from the mind. You will know if certain of these activities will work better, but I recommend starting with only one until you have a well-established habit of being present during this time. When you practice, you will bring all your attention to the thing at hand - focus on the dishwashing rather than what you'll make for dinner tomorrow, what your partner said to upset you, your work project. It is well-documented now that rest makes the mind function better (what they're really saying is resting as Awareness is superior to functioning only from identification with mind), so even if you're on a deadline of some sort, you'll be better off designating this time to mindfulness with the utmost regularity. In so doing, you are also showing the mind your commitment to this process - in a sense, you are exhibiting boundaries to your small self.

Bonus: I have taken to designating the first minute of a shower to cold immersion, and this has proven to be a very effective way of centering. By incorporating slow, deep breaths, you will master the cold, and the cold will become a teacher - you will quickly find that to breathe slowly and relax the bodymind is a world away from chattering one's teeth and complaining. There is nothing like the cold to bring about presence. Wim Hof, the esteemed teacher who has shown the world how to go past the supposed limits of the human bodymind, has many resources on this practice joined with breath and meditative practices, and I credit him with my introduction to it. Providing you don't get wrapped up in the activity itself as a complete cure, this is something you can take as far as you like.

### Sitting Meditation

When you have become accustomed to the practice of doing only one thing at a time, of training the mind on only that one thing, you are practicing living meditation. If you wish to simply continue as is, this will be wonderful for your capacity to knowingly be the Awareness you are. However, I find that sitting meditation adds an element of determination and clarity for the unruly bodymind by creating a situation where we must sit through whatever comes up within the body during our session, and over time, to realize the trends and habits of the mind. Whenever we sit, especially if we are not accustomed to sitting, the whole array of sensations will begin to come up - it might feel hard to breathe, back pain might commandeer all your attention for an entire session, you may notice pains you never knew were there. This is all part of the practice. Many of these pains will subside as you learn to accept their existence, because as acceptance arises, resistance inherently dissolves, and with it much or all of the tension and inflammation that are apparent in the physical layer of the body. However, that tension which does not subside will be welcomed into our experience, and it remains as our tool.

Sitting meditation may not be the ideal starting point for everyone, and if it currently seems that the Divine will that will help you face the entirety of the mind's inner workings is a little spotty or elusive, you may wish to save this practice for when you are prepared to experience your bare mind without any movement or stimuli. It is also important to remember that meditation is something to be celebrated - it is the act of communing with the Divine that you are, of letting all else drop to allow peace to come to the front of your experience. To struggle to make things drop is to try to meditate. When you have actually experienced the *state* of meditation, you will know. Until then, compassion and surrender are key. Starting out with a one hour practice is not necessary and may be detrimental to your enjoyment - knock off that trained intensity and go for five minutes. When five minutes feels comfortable, jump to ten. Whatever is comfortable for you is acceptable. The very popular Transcendental Meditation style is practiced in twenty-minute intervals twice a day, whereas Vipassana Meditation asks for two one-hour sessions a day for the desired effect. Anywhere between the two is a great place to land.

Entire books are written describing how to meditate. Here I will provide you with a bare bones look.

Come to a comfortable position, either lying down, sitting in a chair, or on a cushion in one of the common postures shown below. Find a straight spine, as though you were being held up by a puppeteer (how fitting). Allow the hands to fall where they do naturally, usually at the knees or thighs, depending on your chosen position. If seated, allow the torso to lean just slightly forward, and relax. Specific hand positions are sometimes used, but not necessary.

This is not time to perfect your breathing technique. This is not time to catch up on processing what happened yesterday. Everything outside of the practice of meditation has its own time - this is your time to just be. If you find the mind is really stuck on something, I recommend journaling or free writing a few pages before you begin, so some of that energy can be dissipated.

Begin to notice the body breathing. Notice that the body breathes by itself - the mind could not handle this task and everything else. Breathing is taken care of by Awareness - you. Notice the body breathing itself, and begin to tune into aspects of this. The way the breath feels coming into the nostrils, the change in temperature of the air coming in and out, the way the belly and/or chest move to allow the breath, where the breath ends up at the top of the inhale, whether it is deep or shallow, which nostril is taking in more or all of the breath - all of these are aspects of breath that usually go unnoticed.

While the practice of meditation is extremely simple to understand, the myriad obstacles presented by the mind can seem to occupy us for a lifetime if we let them. As you notice the breath more deeply, many things may arise to bring the attention away from the practice. The mind thinks this is very boring - in truth, it knows that contained within the breath, or any singular or open point of focus, is the quieting of it, and it doesn't want to be quiet - it wants to be relevant at all times, to keep hypnotizing you. When you notice the mind, observe it as you would a dearly loved child - changing every moment, a force unto itself, not you, and holding no real power over you whatsoever. Accept whatever comes - even if you sit for fifteen minutes without a single breath spent in unbroken concentration, you engaged in the practice of meditation. Even when this happens, you may often feel afterward a sense of calm - you have allowed some of the mind's energy to be acknowledged, and you have learned more about its antics. You are beginning to see the separation between it and you. In this practice, as in all things, all is well.

Note: of course you are not "good at" meditation. The mind is the one looking to be good at it. You are exempt from such judgment. Release the idea of performing well or poorly. Notice those thoughts are not you.

### Referring to the Self

Part of the process of coming to experience oneself is to begin to depend upon that self, and to realize that when that self is fully known and depended upon, nothing external is needed. To experience this practice, we first begin to hold our tongue. When we vent, we are exercising the muscle of complaining - of the smaller self finding fault in things. This only attracts more energy to the negative, and while it gives us temporary relief, it makes the complaining muscle stronger. Eckhart Tolle refers to this part of our ego as the pain body, as an entity which seeks to strengthen itself by feeding on your pain. When you feed the pain body your negative thoughts, you reinforce the process - you don't need to believe in this, you can recognize with just a little attention to the complaining voice that it likes to do it. We are working now to minimize that by seeing it as separate from us and by not reacting to it. Instead, we refer to the higher self, draw strength from within, and learn to change our reactive patterns.

An excellent way to learn to contain and redirect energy within you is to begin a journaling practice or to adjust your existing one. Many years ago, I often had the impulse to burn my journals when I reflected back on them, because I saw the self-pitying aspect of me that I was trying to avoid. Instead of simply redirecting our venting to a journal, we journal slowly - we consider what we want to put down on paper, whether the sentiments are lasting or simply need to be transformed under the light of Awareness. When we shine light on the antics of the mind, we weaken them - noticing these antics and deciding that they don't even make today's "me" news is powerful, as long as this comes from discernment and not repression or suppression. In recognizing the falseness of our thoughts in real-time, we do not need to burden others with our complaints nor subject ourselves to the feeling of not being heard by others or not getting our feelings out to our satisfaction. We are in charge of our own process, and we do not waste a morsel of energy feeding negativity. Over time, the entity becomes weak, our discernment grows, and our ability to notice falseness in the mind expands.

### Yoga - A Complete System of Healing

Did you know that physical exercise only comprised three of the 196 aphorisms of The Yoga Sutras of Patanjali, the Divinely inspired work which became the foundation for modern practice? In fact, The

Sutras mainly focused on the moral and personal observances which are the true foundation of a yoga practice, as well as other spiritual aspects of practice. A complete yoga practice includes the moral and personal observances, physical practice, breathwork, the practice of meditation, and the three subsequent states of consciousness that will ensue with progressive and steady practice. Incorporating the first five steps together, the last three naturally unfold until one has cultivated the ability to keep one's attention on the present moment to the point that union with the Divine is experienced continually. That is the true intention of yoga, and physical practice only supports that goal. Learning to eat and maintain the body in a way that supports the mind, understanding the layers of the body more deeply and how the chakras play into overall wellness, and learning the lesser known styles of physical practice which can support you on an "off" day are all ways to go far beyond a simple workout and understanding why yoga has stood the test of time.

In my training to become a yoga teacher, I was exposed to the truth of what we really are more clearly than ever before. I did not know that was what it was when I heard it, and nothing I've read clearly describes Divinity as being the one that I already am - I understood this to be something to strive for. In this, nonduality differs in one very important way, as there is nothing to strive for or to attain, and only one thing to realize for oneself. So, I recommend the practice of yoga *through* a nondual lens - use the realization to inform the practice, and the practice to support deeper resonance.

I like to think of my physical practice as breaking down to these four main styles:

Yang Yoga - stereotypical yoga, a movement-based class designed to get energy through and out

Yin Yoga - a slow practice in which all poses are grounded (not standing or moving). Instrumental in working through physical blockages which may point us to emotional ones

Restorative Yoga - would be considered a "yin" style by definition, but has been given another name for differentiation. A completely restful practice in which we assume poses for fifteen to twenty minutes (three to four poses per class) and support the body with props, allowing for an engaged rest period and profound opening of the body's tissues. Surprisingly to many, this has been shown to support weight regulation as the emotions which hamper the metabolism are worked through and released

Yoga Nidra - as mentioned in the Body Awareness exercise, this practice is excellent for working through emotional blockages, overcoming insomnia, finding relief from PTSD, and gaining body awareness. We can use it to sharpen discernment in releasing attachment to polarizing concepts.

More in-depth information on yoga can be found anywhere you look these days. I recommend using discernment and seeking out no-frills information that honors the lineage and original intention of this method. A fitness-oriented program only gets you about 2% of the way there in terms of conveying the actual information pertaining to awakening. A few sample yoga sequences are on my website.

**What Am I?**

The tradition of self-inquiry is central to recognizing one's true nature. If all other traditions, exercises, and practices are let go of, keep this.

To sit with oneself and simply ask the question, *what am I?* is at the heart of deconstructing the constructed self.

When I ask this question, and perhaps immediately more mental content flows into my attention, I observe this content. Is it me? Did I sign off on it? No, I did not.

Thought after thought, through this process of negation, it becomes very clear - I am not the thoughts. I am not the mind. I am observing the thoughts coming into awareness and falling away.

You will also begin to notice that when your attention remains open, thoughts will begin to lose their sticky quality - here it is, there it goes, and it's gone. And if this is true of thoughts, I see that this must be true of happenings - all that happens, happens. When it's done happening, it's gone.

What you will find with steady attention is that all that is not you no longer captures your attention as it had - this present moment, like one big package, is within attention. When this moment passes, it is gone.

With this simple practice, what you will stumble upon is in fact the deconstruction of all that is false. You will find that this practice injects itself into the One Thing at a Time exercise - all that appears will be recognized as Not Me. It will no longer capture the attention, but simply flow through it. What you will also be doing in this practice is reclaiming your say over your experience - where you place your attention, your energy is plugged. No longer captivated by mind, you will no longer live a life of mind. You will no longer live a life one layer removed, lost in thought. You will live as you.

**Forgiveness - An Experiment in Healing**

Keeping in mind all that we discussed about forgiveness in Chapters 5 and 7, begin to incorporate forgiveness into your daily habits. It is often easier to start with the smaller perceived slights, so notice when you find the mind becoming perturbed over a look from a stranger, being cut off on the road, or an office squabble. Here, we are looking to recognize not only a shared experience of humanity, but a shared participation in this really hard game that we signed up for and are almost all playing out completely asleep. Understanding that one simply does not presently have the capacity to understand what they do from a place of full consciousness, how can we possibly hold their actions against them? They have forgotten they are experiencing a cause and effect machine, just like you were until you realized you were - they truly know not what they do. And, in the understanding that each package of awareness, each soul, may have lived many lives before this one, we can concede that this sliver of Consciousness acting as another human in another life has likely hurt the other sliver of Consciousness in their other life. And yet, at the deepest root of reality, even those two slivers of Consciousness are reunited in the One, and were never hurt.

Say to yourself, "I forgive them, because they don't know what they've done." Or, if you find that you don't know what it means to forgive but you are ready to do it, simply say, "I am now willing to forgive." Notice any changes within the body as you release the emotional energy that would otherwise be spent holding onto resentment - you may notice tingling in your chest or gurgling in your belly if a release occurs, in which case, notice over the coming days any improvement in functionality of the heart, lungs, or digestive system. Keep practicing this until it becomes easy and automatic to forgive, and when any stories arise in an effort to hold the resentment to you, recognize the limiting belief that is the foundation for the story. Remember, others do not need to adhere to your way of seeing things, and in the end, nobody is going to see everything exactly the way you do - so you might as well scrap the whole idea of holding others to your standards. The ease and flow that will follow dropping the entire system you have used to judge so-called "others" will be plenty of motivation to carry this practice into your deeper and older wounds.

*Bonus: Ho'oponopono*

The Hawaiian tradition of ho'oponopono has gained some popularity in recent years, and this prayer covers all bases in the situation of perceived slights. In this instance, we recognize that in a past life we may have transgressed against a so-called other, and we say or pray to them, "I'm sorry, please forgive me, thank you, I love you." This is commonly used as a mantra, said over and over, and used to restore wellness and happiness in addition to mitigating conflict.

**Perspective: Awareness**

In the next and final three exercises, we will practice shifting our perspective just slightly so that we are looking through the appropriate lens to see what has been in front of us our entire lives. When our minds zoom in on one thing and chatter on, we miss the millions of other things - more importantly, we miss the cohesion of all things. As Awareness, we allow ourselves to absorb the whole picture. This is how life becomes magical and we change the story of our life circumstances. As we get comfortable with each of these exercises, we will notice a space widening between the mind and the true "I." In this space, we will notice many things that went unnoticed before - including a subtle tingling in every part of the body, actually the energetic layer of the body and the sign that alerted the deeply meditating Buddha to the fact that all in the world of form is impermanent and reforming itself every single second. As we deepen this experience, we become more and more attentive to our true nature.

*Changing Lenses*

I like to think of this exercise as changing from glasses to contact lenses - one minute you can only see what fits within the glass lenses directly in front of you. The next minute, you can see with the entirety of your peripheral vision. We can incorporate our other senses into this exercise as well.

Right now you are likely experiencing looking through a pair of eyes and hearing with a pair of ears. These organs are part of the vehicle you experience to drive around this earth: the bodymind. Without you, the eyes would have nowhere to transmit the images they pick up. Without the eyes, you as Awareness would not see. However, these two are not the same. You are experiencing the visual aspect of the illusion through the eyes of the body, but the eyes are not part of the essential you.

All your life you have thought you were looking through your eyes, but they are on loan. Right now, as you soften your gaze and look around the room, notice that you register what is coming in through the eyes just an instant before the mind begins to narrate to you what you are seeing. Further, recognizing this simple, subtle but powerful truth - you don't need it narrated to you. The idea that a voice in the head is describing everything that is happening just becomes another hilarious joke when you realize you never needed it to; you as Awareness are able to understand the entire picture without it being interpreted for you. Begin to witness through the eyes and notice what is there without any commentary. Does the picture change? It may help to imagine yourself as your friendly local spirit animal - does your cat require words to understand what the eyes see? As you look out through the eyes, make the subtle shift of simply noticing - using the vehicle to see, being the alien inside the human suit. In doing this, there will no longer be a hyper focus on apparently individual items in the illusion - the whole thing is a cohesive movie appearing on the screen of life. Where is the screen? What is the screen? It is the space uniting all the apparently individual things - it is you.

*Rephrase Game*

Until now, when you have felt various emotions coming up and through the experience via the body, the mind has latched onto each one of these and attached it to its identity. "I am sad, I am hungry." When that feeling passes, you are still here. If you were the feeling, you would be gone. So, what is a more accurate way to state the experience? As an experience! When we rephrase the mind's narrations, we take one step in removing the true Self from the picture of suffering. After all, the true "I" doesn't suffer a single bit, and when human speech comes closer to reflecting that, we shift the ideas we have allowed the mind to perpetuate.

When any negative feeling comes up, become accustomed to thinking and saying, "I'm noticing anger coming up." "The mind is telling a story about going crazy." Similar to the way in which the therapeutic technique of labeling our feelings can help dissipate them, rephrasing our feelings to create space between the "I" that is watching them unfold and the "me" that is acting them out, we disempower the feelings over our experience and empower ourselves - I am Awareness, I don't go crazy! I don't get angry or hold resentment. I am love itself, endless joy, and incapable of being lonely. I am just here observing the world of form; I am experiencing emotions, but not being them.

Another way to apply this game, and one which I practiced unknowingly for years before awakening, is what I call the Editing Game. When you hear yourself saying or thinking something, begin to continually edit it until you've arrived at a correct statement. *I'm not good at starting new habits - no that's not true, new habits are hard to start - no, that doesn't have to be true, the challenge is in our habitual patterns, but that's not unique to me - so, habits are only hard to start when we are in our own way which is a form of societal conditioning, not personal to me.* Suddenly, starting a new habit is easy, because there are no limitations in place around it. The process becomes lighter and easier just from the thought shift. Note: I don't recommend playing this game out loud in multiple layers in conversation, unless your partner is onto the game.

*The Guessing Game*

Perhaps the most powerful tool I use today to bring focus to only one thing at a time is one I stumbled upon in my younger years. Having had the experience of what would be called undiagnosed ADHD, a seeming epidemic today, my report cards always indicated a difficulty concentrating and a surplus of energy. However, I have vivid memories of staring up at the moon for long periods, noticing its variations in color and texture, or becoming engrossed in books for hours. I believe going undiagnosed was a great gift to me in terms of growth potential - I never identified with this tendency, and continued to think of it as something I could investigate and work with, rather than something I was stuck with or that could only be corrected chemically. If your ability to focus varies from activity to activity and with different stress levels... ask yourself what is really at the root of this, and why a chemical imbalance only affects certain activities.

Today, when I am listening to a respected teacher and noticing the mind is throwing up the obstacle of diverting my attention from information that, if taken in deeply, would pose a threat to the overinflated importance of the mind, I do one simple thing: I guess what the speaker will say next.

In this subtle activity, the attention is fixed fully on the words of my friend, teacher, or what is happening in the present moment. Rather than living in the mode of the mind, which likes to think it knows how the world works, I shift into the curiosity and innocence of a child simply by taking greater interest in what is actually happening than the mind's commentary on it. This can take a little practice, and at first may feel a little strained, but once you have found the appropriate calibration of effortless yet focused attention, you will know from the complete lack of commentary that you can use this one simple shift to listen and observe as the Awareness that you truly are, rather than secondhand through the commentary of the mind. This simple activity will begin to feel like meditation, and over time will result in a strong shift in perspective from watching the movie of life with commentary from multiple actors at once to the peace of simply allowing it to unfold on-screen.

# CHAPTER TEN

## ONE THING AT A TIME

**Who Are We and What Are We Doing Here?**
Each human being is a projection of the one creative force behind and within the entire Universe of form. As such, each contains the equipment necessary to create, and to generate pure joy in the contribution to the collective dream, and to embody pure and selfless love. However, this human is just the equipment - the capacity for love, creativity, and joy all come from Awareness, using various tools to act out this expression. The self that most of us think we are is another collective creation - the "me" the mind thinks I am is just a collection of thoughts, beliefs and experiences had pertaining to this particular bodymind. And ultimately, the only thing creating the experience of separation from oneself is the belief in the mind as oneself. This false belief is behind all the division and suffering in the entire world - if we knew we were all ultimately the very same, with no separate bodies and no beliefs, there would be no reason to take so seriously the happenings in the illusory world of form.

Humans exist to enable Consciousness to show itself to itself through mirroring. Consciousness had the idea to create the world, and from that idea, that "word," the world was created. Imbued with creative power via Consciousness, humans act out the power of the word as well, but it is subject to the physics of this dream. Consciousness uses this world as a contrast to itself - the world of form is everything that Consciousness is *not*, and yet there are glimpses of pure and innocent Consciousness wherever we look. It is the sole purpose of each human life to discover the Divinity within and behind it - one's occupation or way of spending time and doing things on earth is just another vehicle through which the one purpose is fulfilled.

### Continuing the Journey

As you continue your journey to the center of yourself, you will begin to see the world differently. Many will begin to see the Divinity and "sensitive soul" within animals and may choose to eat only plants - or rather, suddenly the interest in meat is gone. Some will wish to change careers, becoming coaches, teachers, and other kinds of "helpers," but there is no attachment to this as an identity or an obligation. Plenty simply choose to apply love and presence to what they are already experiencing. You may find that you wish to rid yourself of clutter as you become more attuned to the energy around you, that certain kinds of dramatic television simply no longer bring satisfaction as a sense of lack diminishes and no longer needs filled, or that you no longer see the need to impress others or engage in conflict.

The wonderful thing about this path is that it is entirely self-made - there is no way for me or anyone else to tell you what you should or shouldn't do. Even extremely seasoned teachers will disagree on certain aspects of the path, paving the way for all students to do the same. Awakening to the truth of reality, also called enlightenment, does not mean you have all the answers to life's problems - it means you're okay with not having all the answers, because you know who you truly are, and that you were enlightened all along. In this way, all pressure to emulate, adore, or revere our teachers above others is completely removed - they are us.

### Group Effort, Solo Effort

One's individual journey is entirely led by themselves - to simply follow in another's footsteps will only get you so far, and ultimately lead you to a moment when you must choose, in the words of sociologist and teacher Brené Brown, the way of the wilderness - happily going alone into solitude. It is entirely up to you whether you will hold yourself accountable from moment to moment for the unhappiness that has resulted from your believing things about yourself that are not true. If you think you can't handle that journey, that is the small self talking, and the root of the whole issue - you are Consciousness itself, there is no doubt that you can do it should you choose to consent to a new way of playing the game of life.

While each soul is having their own experience which no other can walk for them, we are also on a collective journey - as Ram Dass said, we are all walking each other home. Every little thing that makes us feel bad was placed there for us to eventually come to realize that suffering is no longer necessary in life, that we can ride each wave and let it pass. Every challenging human can be thanked for the feelings that have arisen in the mind that are leading you to walk away from old patterns that led to suffering.

Awakening is coming about in more dramatic ways at this time. While unconsciousness is on the rise with some spending entire days in front of screens unaware of their surroundings or feelings, more people than ever are realizing that this is not their true nature, are turning from society's dream and creating their own. More people are awakening than ever and there are more teachers, more ways of teaching, and more varied results as our life experiences give us very different kinds and degrees of egos to work through. When Consciousness shifts to a great enough scale, Consciousness at the deepest and most collective level will also awaken from the dream it is having. This is the meaning of the Sanskrit term *moksha* and of the return of God in religious texts. While the Universe can have an expiration date, we do not - we are that which preceded it, and we will still be, as one, if this Universe is no more.

**Meeting Resistance With Love**

In addition to the resistance we may encounter within the ego and the physical body, we may encounter resistance from outside the body. This could come from family members who wish us to stay the way we are or don't understand as we drop our belief systems, stop feeling upset about things happening around us, or even lovingly create distance between ourselves and others. Acquaintances whose egos sense "danger" in the form of the Consciousness that is capable of dissolving them might lash out or avoid it. Even strangers who see your peace as suspect in the seeming absence of their own might offer a side-eye glance. You may find that your employer places demands on you which no longer suit you, or maybe the old activities you enjoyed, like serial dating or heavy drinking, just don't make you feel a false high anymore and you no longer need them. In some cases, as in my own, relationships dissolve, entire career paths change, one may find themselves quite alone temporarily, with one's life circumstances seemingly disintegrated; in only a short time after these periods of transition, the entire thing is rebuilt better than one small human could have imagined.

In many religions, this is known as God testing the faith of followers. In nonduality, this is the Universe acting in accordance with Divine will, helping us to fine-tune, to rid our experience of the things which no longer serve our journey, and to strengthen our resolve. Once we choose the path, the path chooses us.

Knowing this, when these obstacle-like gifts appear to us, we can begin to welcome them with love. We can understand why some may not want this change for us - we ourselves experienced egoic resistance in it and perhaps quite a lot of it, outweighed only by some tingly sense that we needed to pursue this further. In Western and scientific terms, this seems flimsy. So, we can reserve judgment when others judge, we can keep our eyes to our own path, and keep in our attention the peace of which we have only seen glimmers at this point in life. The more grounded we become in this peace, the more compelling it will be to others.

**Delighting in the World**

We did not come here to save each other - the life in each human experience is representative of ourself, that sliver of Consciousness we presently have filtered access to. We are capable of liberating our experience from suffering by referring inwardly, and it is the only way. In the end, this only affects the experience of the outer world - all is well with me no matter what. Knowing this, we can take the weight of the world off our shoulders and delight in all we see. Whatever happens in this world of form is a reflection of the degree of individual and collective Consciousness, and when the dream is over, all of this will have never existed in literal terms. It has existed within the collective mind, but once it is over, there will be no trace. Like the scene in "Harry Potter and the Deathly Hallows," when Harry asks Dumbledore if his white-light-post-death-limbo-dream is real or in his mind, and Dumbledore replies, "of course it's in your mind, Harry! Why should that mean that it isn't real?" This present moment, this thing happening right now, is the only real thing. Past and present are not here, do not exist - they exist only as constructs in the mind, and only because they are believed.

Knowing all of this, and without any attachment to the bodymind, we can use our exploration vehicle to see all we wish, with no yearning for more or grasping our gifts tightly. We allow all to rise and fall, we experience joy which has no cause and so cannot be interrupted by change. Underpinning all of this is a peace that makes up the fabric of reality, with everything existing within it. This peace is ours the moment we take it. There isn't going to be a reason to be happy - to look for these reasons is a detour. We are already the source of happiness itself - we simply remove the obstacles to it, becoming less of what we are not so that the true self can flood the form which we inhabit. It is then that our life circumstances become the heart of zen, nirvana, and heaven on earth - doing one thing, joyfully, happily, at a time.

## Parting Thoughts

While teaching a business course for future Licensed Massage Therapists, I stumbled upon something fascinating in the text which I was meant to disseminate. It was a description of marketing, and it went something like this: "marketing is the process of identifying consumers' wants and needs; of maximizing pleasure and minimizing displeasure."

Somehow I had stumbled upon something astounding - this textbook was admitting, right there without disguise, that marketing was the enemy of human happiness. How was it doing that?

Once again, the Four Noble Truths of Buddhism state that in life there is suffering; that the cause of this suffering is attachment to life going a certain way for us, or in other words, the aversion to pain and the clinging to pleasure; that there is a way out; that the way out is through purification of the bodymind by following the Eightfold Path, learning to release the constructed self and be as one truly is. This textbook was inadvertently confirming that marketing, something today's humans can hardly escape on any given day, is only feeding this imbalance.

This helped me see so clearly how nothing is wrong with me, or with any individual - somehow, each human is playing its part, powered by the attention of Awareness on personhood and its resulting thoughts, in solidifying concepts around life that just aren't true. The solution to this is simply to drop them. All of this writing and reading, all of the seeking, and we've come to realize that the path is entailed simply in the dropping of extraneous beliefs - when we do, all that can possibly be left is the truth of who we are. We are not required to adopt any spiritual beliefs in order to allow this to unfold -

we must simply prefer the truth to falseness via opinions and unverifiable beliefs. We must simply consent to a new story, one that will differ from the one perpetuated by the world of form. We must be willing to brave the loneliness that is perpetuated by our false belief of separation until we come to understand that we have never been alone.

In this journey, the body is our vessel, our vehicle, and our tool. It tells us when we're off track, it rejoices when we rejoice. It presents negative feedback both when we are in danger and when we are off track in perceiving danger; it is up to us to discern the difference and reconcile our understanding so that the physical body works in harmony with the mind's processes once again.

A friend of mine told me that in all his years, while he absolutely believes that enlightenment exists, he doesn't believe that it is continuous in a single person - that "even Eckhart Tolle has to make a sandwich." The belief here is that when we are obliged to function as the character we play, we drop the peace or characterlessness that we have been attempting to cultivate, however ardently. Of course, if you've read closely you'll retort, "if you've dropped the idea that you're separate, making a sandwich just becomes a thing the human aspect does, which you are simply and knowingly observing!" And you'd be correct. Even if the character of "you" spends half the day angry or anxious, there is an aspect within that is observing this unperturbed - that is You. When you know this, making a sandwich does not interrupt this new understanding. When you truly embrace this, the anger and anxiety will not stand over time, and they will become less and less a part of the human aspect as the one truly in charge takes the reins. Indeed, even having quite a busy schedule does not take away from the fact that underneath all of this is the fabric that holds it all together, and that fabric, that Consciousness, You, does not ever cease to be peace itself, the non-doing non-entity which subtly shines through the characters in this crazy world. Continuous enlightenment is who you really are; to experience it in the dream is simply to never forget that you are That.

On your journey, I wish you great humor. When you're staring up at the trees and suddenly realize they are of you, and also that you are none of this, and you begin to simultaneously experience joy, relief, sadness, and that familiar voice wondering if your neighbors or passersby can see you crying and lifting your arms to the sky, it helps to be able to laugh at yourself on top of it all. To laugh at the entire premise of this game-like thing we are doing, seemingly abounding with suffering and yet insubstantial and entirely subject to our understanding, is to become a knowingly enlightened one - a Buddha.

I wish you the kind of imperfect teachers who still get the message across - who recognize the unhealed in themselves and spare others from it. While our teachers may know the one Truth, they may still be grappling with the vestiges of an immense ego, playing the same tricks on them as you. An enlightened being loves the imperfect within the world of form - allowing the world into your heart, allowing love to arise where all judgment, seemingly protecting us, used to be, is to allow enlightenment to merge with human experience. As we excavate our way to the one Truth together, as we walk each other home, I send you the prayer of lovingkindness. Be happy, for that is what you are; be healthy, for that flows naturally from your unfiltered light; be free from danger, as you have always been as the undying source of all life and love; live with ease, as your essential self has always done.

## ONE THING AT A TIME

# ABOUT THE AUTHOR

Heather Ralston is a teacher of nonduality. She began her journey with the practice of intuitive bodywork, meditation, and yoga, eventually finding answers through intensive self-study. Heather lives in Dayton, Ohio.

Made in the USA
Las Vegas, NV
05 March 2025